Helping Children and Teens with Difficult-to-Treat OCD

by the same author

The No Worries Guide to Raising Your Anxious Child
A Handbook to Help You and Your Anxious Child Thrive
Karen Lynn Cassiday
ISBN 978 1 78775 887 2
eISBN 978 1 78775 888 9

of related interest

The A–Z Guide to Exposure
Creative Exposure and Response Prevention Activities
for 70+ Childhood Fears and Worries
Dawn Huebner and Erin Neely
ISBN 978 1 83997 322 2
eISBN 978 1 83997 323 9

OCD – Tools to Help You Fight Back!
A CBT Manual for Therapists
Cynthia Turner, Georgina Krebs and Chloë Volz
Illustrated by Lisa Jo Robinson
ISBN 978 1 84905 403 4
eISBN 978 0 85700 771 1

OCD – Tools to Help You Fight Back!
A CBT Workbook for Young People
Cynthia Turner, Georgina Krebs and Chloë Volz
Illustrated by Lisa Jo Robinson
ISBN 978 1 84905 402 7
eISBN 978 0 85700 770 4

Breaking Free from OCD
A CBT Guide for Young People and Their Families
Jo Derisley, Isobel Heyman, Sarah Robinson and Cynthia Turner
ISBN 978 1 84310 574 9
eISBN 978 1 84642 799 2

HELPING CHILDREN AND TEENS WITH DIFFICULT-TO-TREAT OCD

A Guide to Treating Scrupulosity, Existential, Relationship, Harm, and Other OCD Subtypes

Karen Lynn Cassiday

Jessica Kingsley Publishers
London and Philadelphia

First published in Great Britain in 2023 by Jessica Kingsley Publishers
An imprint of John Murray Press

1

Copyright © Karen Lynn Cassiday 2023

A CIP catalogue record for this title is available from the
British Library and the Library of Congress

ISBN 978 1 83997 442 7
eISBN 978 1 83997 443 4

Printed and bound in the United States by Integrated Books International

Jessica Kingsley Publishers' policy is to use papers that are natural, renewable and recyclable products and made from wood grown in sustainable forests. The logging and manufacturing processes are expected to conform to the environmental regulations of the country of origin.

Jessica Kingsley Publishers
Carmelite House
50 Victoria Embankment
London EC4Y 0DZ

www.jkp.com

John Murray Press
Part of Hodder & Stoughton Limited
An Hachette UK Company

Contents

Introduction

I went to graduate school when exposure with response prevention (ERP) was a brand-new therapy that shocked the mental health world because it was so effective and unusual compared with the standard talking therapy. When I first heard about ERP for obsessive compulsive disorder (OCD), I was excited. I loved the idea of directly teaching a patient how to face their fears. The treatment seemed so practical. Better yet, it worked so rapidly compared to every other known treatment. When I got to work with my first contamination OCD patient, I was thrilled to see how a homebound patient who could not touch anything restored his mental health in a matter of weeks just because we did every possible thing to have him touch and endure contamination until it got easy. It was just like the cases my advisor described. The second, third and fourth patients were similarly miraculous in their recoveries from ordering, checking and contamination OCD. I felt so accomplished and honored to be part of such a therapeutic revolution. This idyllic phase of having wild successes lasted for the next six months until I encountered a patient with a different kind of OCD, the kind that had the patient obsessing about whether, or not, they had told the truth. What happened next was a lesson in professional humility.

I did what many do. I assumed that I and ERP were up to the job, and I expected rapid improvement. No research had yet been done that described the variation in treatment response for different subtypes of OCD. The term scrupulosity was still understood to be the word Catholics used to describe unnecessary religious compulsions. I made a hierarchy of exposure situations that began with something that I thought would be easy. Tell a white lie. I then spent the next several sessions with the patient getting stuck repeatedly on fruitless discussion of the rationale for white lies (deliberate deception done for the benefit of others) versus lying for self-gain. I got caught up in attempts to use cognitive therapy that only led to back and forth debate about the morality of ERP when it involves lying of any kind. I tried persuading the patient to just try the exposure to see what happened without getting stuck on morality, but to no avail. I was dead in the water and every bit of advice my supervisor gave me did not seem to gain any traction. I was stuck and my patient was stuck, even though I had this supposedly fabulous therapy. What was wrong? With me? With ERP? With my patient? The final straw was when I left work late, a half day after I had seen my patient only to see her repeatedly going back to the security guard to say something, then leaving and then stopping and going back again. The look on the security guard's face said it all, "This must be one of the patients from the mental health clinic! Help!" I went over, pulled my patient aside and discovered that she had been compulsively trying to say "Goodbye" to the security guard but was not sure she really meant it so she was compulsively going back to tell the guard that she was not sure she was sincere and then doubted the sincerity of that response, and over and over and over. I pulled her out of the building, realizing that I had failed at helping her. Our clinic policy of dropping patients from treatment who were unable to engage in the response prevention portion of treatment after three slips meant that she soon discontinued treatment. Now what?

Since that time I was overwhelmed by this young woman's OCD, the field of treatment for OCD has grown. Refinements in how to conceptualize ERP, cognitive therapy, metacognitive therapy, self-compassion therapy, mindfulness-based approaches, transcranial magnetic stimulation, medications and more have provided additional tools for those who treat OCD. The dilemma remains, however, that some subtypes of OCD are much more difficult to treat than others. Certain subtypes of OCD—the ones covered in this book—continue to frustrate therapists because the types of obsessions and compulsions in these subtypes contain subtleties of symptom presentation that relate to nuances in managing intolerance of uncertainty, differential diagnosis and grasp of cultural and theological concepts that are difficult to access. My clinical experience and the developing field of research and treatment on difficult-to-treat variations in OCD have shown me that a willingness to be patient, persistent and scrappy will serve you well in the long run.

What do I mean by being scrappy? I mean being willing to let go of your preconceived idea of what should happen in treatment. Scrappy means refocusing on the big ideas of mental wellness and doing whatever works instead of getting stuck on what does not work. For example, many therapists get stuck when a patient or their parents, mentors or support system dictates that things seemingly good exposure practice is unacceptable. Families and patients may decide to end treatment before they reach the therapeutic goal you had in mind, when they are in less pain as opposed to being truly well. Patients may also refuse opportunities for treatment because they repeatedly find information that supports the continuation of their reassurance seeking, rituals and avoidance. The internet, support groups and parental and cultural overprotection of children, advocacy for the marginalized and the moral pressure to become "woke" can intensify the problem. What do you do when your patient tells you they feel it is immoral to have fun because the state of the world is so terrible? You might accidentally feel as if you are in a cage match with OCD, culture and your own response to the deep moral divides of religion, politics, gender awareness, global warming and more. How do you respond when a teen challenges your suggestion for doing imaginal exposure by challenging your morality, "Implicit bias is what keeps privileged people like you in power and continues the oppression! You don't get it. I have had it so much easier than others and I should never get used to it or feel less concerned"? What do you do when you ask a teen to sit with their uncertainty obsessions about gender identity by imagining never knowing for sure what their gender identity might be and then discover that all their friends identify themselves as being demi-girl, pansexual, trans, demi-queer, neither male nor female and more? What do you do when a patient's family asks you about your personal faith experience to determine their comfort level with working with you? How you handle these kinds of situations can make all the difference between the growth of your patient, and premature dropout and defeat.

This book summarizes the work of many and my own clinical experience to help you better wrestle with these challenging OCD subtypes and the clinical dilemmas they generate with competence and confidence. I will cover how to assess and manage the typical dilemmas that challenge all therapists who work with these difficult subtypes by covering the following topics in the upcoming chapters: handling oppositional behaviors, religious scrupulosity, moral scrupulosity, OCD about sexuality and gender identity, existential OCD, relationship-focused OCD, self-harm-focused OCD and avoiding therapist burnout. My hope is that you will be better prepared to help your patients find their way to mental wellness amid their obsessions and compulsions no matter what their symptom presentation might be.

A note to the reader

All case examples of patients have been altered to maintain privacy and confidentiality. Identifying information has been changed and, in some cases, composite examples have been created to help hide identity and clarify the clinical example.

It is also understood that all children, teens and young adults may have various presentations of gender identity and self-expressed pronouns to reference their identity. For the sake of implication, this text will refer to the wide variety of gender identities using he/her, they/them and she/he, understanding that many other pronouns and self-identifiers exist as an appropriate expression of gender and non-gender.

To make the text easier to read, "parent" will refer to all types of parents and caregivers who raise children with OCD. It is understood that a wide range of genetic relatives and volunteers devote their lives to raising children whether or not they use the title parent.

Additionally, "patient" will refer to young children through to emerging adults. When a specific reference to an age group is necessary, this reference will be clarified to avoid confusion for the reader.

I recognize my limitations in expressing many nuances of spirituality, faith, morality and religion and acknowledge that my clinical examples and the words used for recommended treatment may not fully express the rich diversity in language and thought that various cultures and subcultures use to address these issues. My hope is that you will be inspired to improve on my understanding as you seek to alleviate the suffering that OCD causes in youth.

To help you better learn the interventions described in this book, each chapter has a video demonstration of some of the more challenging interventions. You can find these videos by going to https://library.jkp.com/redeem using the code ZVEAZDD.

CHAPTER 1

Setting the Stage for Success

What comes to mind when you think about treating obsessive compulsive disorder? For many, it is exposure and response prevention and images of youth who are afraid of contamination or who get stuck with issues of perfection in their schoolwork, clothing or ordering their belongings. There is much more to treating OCD than working with contamination, perfectionism, checking, symmetry or ordering. OCD has infinite variety that can challenge the most experienced clinician because obsessions and compulsions can be unique and focus on topics that are sensitive or difficult to understand.

Research on treatment of OCD shows us that the first-line treatment for OCD in children, teens and emerging adults is exposure with response prevention (O'Kearney, Anstey & von Sanden, 2006). We know that ERP is effective, can obtain rapid results and works especially well for obsessions and compulsions that manifest in behaviors such as washing, ordering, asking questions, repeating, counting. We see that when the compulsions, or rituals, involve immediate consequences and concerns, then ERP is easier to implement and creates an instant mini self-experiment for the patient in handling the situation. For example, when a patient fears getting germs on their hands or mouth because they're afraid of illness, or dread the experience of anxiety or disgust that being dirty entails, they can directly learn to tolerate and recover from getting dirty. All they must do is get dirty. Compare that to being afraid of losing God's approval and missing out on Heaven after death. How do you do exposure to something that can only be experienced after death and that has such eternal consequences? Or how do you do exposure feeling uncertain about your sexuality, or morals?

Easier-to-treat subtypes of OCD (contamination and washing/ avoiding, symmetry and ordering, perfectionism and avoiding mistakes/overworking, just right and doing the opposite) all have a common feature (Williams *et al.*, 2014). They involve easy-to-detect situations that trigger obsessions. Obsessions are often clear-cut and involve a single external and observable circumstance that triggers the obsession and an easy-to-define behavioral experiment that counteracts the compulsion and is the opposite of what the obsession dictates. For example, a patient fears getting sticky hands and avoids any activity that might make them encounter sticky substances or sticky-feeling things. Exposure then becomes putting sticky things on their hands, touching potentially sticky or known sticky surfaces and deliberately making their belongings sticky. The response prevention involves avoiding washing, avoiding using barriers to touch things and immediate recontamination after bathing with maple syrup and glue sticks. This is pretty simple for the patient, the parents and the therapist to grasp and execute. It is easy to verify if the patient's hands are sticky and easy to make sure they do not slip off and wash. You can lock up the soap, even turn off the water main and clearly determine when the child is doing exposure and response prevention. If the obsession involves harming, then often it is easy to disprove the effect of preventing the compulsion (i.e., checking, thinking a bad thought, because failure to do the compulsion results in the immediately observable effect of no harm). For example, I can say aloud, "I hope my children are kidnapped, assaulted and murdered because I forgot to say, 'I love you' this morning," and then go home to discover obviously safe children. I can quickly see that my awful thought has no effect on what happens to my children.

What happens, however, when the obsession involves taking perspective or inferring intention? What do you do when the ritual involves socially acceptable behaviors, such as being kind, polite, thoughtful or faithful? How can you be sure that a child's theological question is a ritual as opposed to being a genuine question, especially when you know that the question is one that everyone asks? What happens when the consequence is far in the future? What do you do when science or theology has no clear answers for the dilemmas that get entangled in your patient's OCD? For example, a patient who obsesses about the sincerity of her commitment to Christ has a double-edged problem. What is the knife edge between acknowledging one's own human status of never being able to be perfectly sincere in any situation and knowing that part of the Christian journey is to continually improve sensitivity to the awareness of God and the ability to love God, others and oneself? Trying to figure out how to define what constitutes exposure can get complicated. Trying to help a patient think about the universal problem of accepting uncertainty and risk-taking gets tricky, especially when each word you say triggers a new anxiety response because anything associated with the topic of their obsession and compulsion sets off more anxiety and even panic. To help you make sense of the landscape for treatment with these types of patients, I will review some basic concepts of high-quality ERP and OCD recovery. These will enable you to better organize your approach to intervention when you are faced with the following subtypes that many clinicians find difficult to treat: scrupulosity-based OCD, that can range from matters of religion to climate change to social justice and morality; LGBTQ+ (lesbian, gay, bisexual, transgender, queer and questioning) OCD; existential OCD; relationship OCD; and self-harming and other harming forms of OCD. Each of these subtypes gets tangled in the intersection between culture, intolerance of uncertainty and nuances of treatment. The following chapters will enable you to develop a clear idea of the goals for treatment that help the patient grow while simultaneously aligning with important cultural values and the science of recovery.

The big picture: The long-term goal for OCD treatment

It is easy to forget that the purpose of treatment is not just to get the patient to do exposure with response prevention or just to do the activities that OCD interrupts or prevents. The goal is much bigger than eliminating symptoms. The goal for every patient with OCD is to learn to quickly recognize when anxiety, obsessive urges, thoughts, images or ideas occur and then to disregard them because they are understood to be a product of their mind. Their goal is to learn to do what the other 96.5 percent of the population does when they experience unwanted intrusive thoughts because they perceive them to be benign (Barrera

& Norton, 2011). Exposure with response prevention is a particularly effective tool for achieving this goal. Other interventions, however, can also work, such as medication, cognitive therapy, acceptance and commitment therapy, unified protocol for anxiety, mindfulness training, attention control training, metacognitive therapy, transcranial magnetic stimulation, deep brain stimulation devices, psychosurgery, novel use of medications such as opiates, medical treatment for pediatric autoimmune neuropsychiatric disorders, or PANS for short, and more (Pittenger *et al.*, 2005). No matter what the type or proposed mechanism of intervention, the long-term goal is the same—to help the patient learn to think, interpret and act like those who do not have OCD. Successful treatment teaches the patient skills of acceptance and tolerance of anxiety, ability to do valued goal-directed behaviors despite the occurrence of obsessions and to learn to ignore obsessions. ERP appears to offer a greater degree of success because the patient repeatedly encounters the thoughts, images and sensations they fear without giving in to compulsions or avoidance. The patient has a direct learning experience that counters their belief that they are unable to cope in the face of obsessions. It builds their belief and skill in alternative healthy coping. Once you recognize this fact, you will have a compass to help you navigate the maze of conceptual and theoretical pitfalls that make it difficult to help difficult-to-treat patients. The goal is not to get patients to decide that their obsessions are acceptable or tolerable. It is to help them recognize that no matter how disturbing their obsession, it is an insignificant experience that demands only a switch in focus to something worthwhile and to proceed as though all is well. That is what people without OCD do. This is what we want our patients to accomplish, regardless of their age or level of anxiety. It sounds simple and it is, unless you get side-tracked by accidentally wrestling with the content of the patient's OCD instead of teaching the patient how to recognize their OCD and learn alternative responses that sidestep rituals, reassurance seeking and avoidance. So, let's discuss the steps you can take to promote success in your difficult-to-treat patients.

Step 1: Remember that some subtypes make it impossible for the patient to feel ready to begin treatment

The effect of anxiety on the human mind and body can be confusing and dismaying. Having a clear understanding of how the human mind prioritizes information and responds to negative reinforcement and how children born into anxiety-prone families are subject to learning conditions that make it easier to develop and maintain OCD symptoms will help you to avoid accidental discouragement. It is easy to forget the effect of the aforementioned when your patient agrees they have OCD and then refuses to engage in treatment. For example, I recall working with a patient whose symptoms consisted of having to perfectly ascertain if they really meant what they said and if they really were correctly saying what they meant. They were bright, articulate and made good grades in school. They had read up on OCD on the internet, helped their parents find my clinic and explained that they wanted to do exposure with response prevention. The first 30 minutes of our first session were excruciating because they never made it past the first explanation of their symptoms. They kept pausing to consider what they were about to say and then offered up several slightly different variations of an answer, then retracted the answer and began again. When their parents interrupted, they got irritated, saying the interruption made them confused and forget what they were about to say. They did this despite their parents' reassurance that they were articulate and had an intact memory. They did this despite me giving them permission to be less exact. Our conversation went something like this:

> Therapist: "Sounds as if you are constantly trying to verify that you are absolutely correct in what you are saying and your OCD makes you worry you have not covered all the details perfectly. Your OCD is so busy being sure, that it makes it difficult to even remember what you just said."
>
> Patient (with a big smile): "That's right! It's like I have to say everything perfectly and never make a mistake and then I can't exactly recall what I just said and I have to say it again to make sure. Now, did I tell you that sometimes I can remember what

I said and I still have to go over it even though I know that I know it? Maybe I am making this up and I don't really have OCD. Sometimes I do really know it and then other times I get really mixed up."

Therapist: "Looks as if you just got hit by another doubting obsession when you described your obsession. Since that keeps happening and seems like the biggest thing that bothers you, can I ask you about other symptoms that kids with OCD might get?"

Patient: "Now, what I was trying to make clear was that I get stuck making sure I say the right thing. Sometimes I get really confused and I have to just keep saying it a different way until I get it right. I am not sure if I really remember what I just thought and said or if I am just making it up."

Therapist: "You have given me a really good description of your OCD and I am confident that you really do have OCD. I want to find out about other possible symptoms, just to be thorough. Have you ever had a time that didn't have to do with your OCD, where you felt sad, couldn't enjoy any of the things you usually liked and felt like nothing mattered to you?"

Patient: "What were you saying before, about my OCD? Are you sure that you understand that I am not sure I said it right? I didn't say it right. I try to be careful and make sure that I describe things exactly as I mean them, but then the second after I say them, I am not sure I said it right and I cannot even be sure I remember right. I am not even sure if I really do have OCD. Do you get that?"

I realized at this point that nothing I or the parents could say would reassure the patient . Their mind was just too busy focusing on obsessive doubt, excessive explanations and reviewing memories. I realized that I was going to have to take a different approach if I wanted to finish the assessment and get started with treatment. I had to accept that OCD was hijacking the session and the patient was therefore unable to stop responding with compulsions. I also realized that it would be very difficult for this patient to begin treatment, because they wanted to feel certain I had the right diagnosis and treatment, which would be impossible to feel because of the nature of their OCD. I have learned from a long history of mistakes that it is pointless to reassure OCD or to give in to its demands in the hope of getting a few moments of cooperation. So, I tried a different approach that I hoped would role model how to respond to constant compulsive statements and questions. I told them, "Looks as if your OCD is hijacking everything you think and say that feels important. I do not want to accidentally make your OCD worse by giving in to its every demand for clarity and certainty. I would like for you to be quiet, so you do not have to give in to your OCD all the time. I know that this will make you feel uncomfortable, and it will be an exposure and response prevention practice for you. I will ask your parents to give me answers and you just give me a thumbs up if you sort of agree or a thumbs down if you sort of disagree with their answer. I don't need perfectly precise answers from you because I can already tell that your OCD is a real tyrant. We are going to practice not knowing things for sure right now by assuming that we will all figure this out as we work together to help you. How does that sound, a thumbs up or a thumbs down?" Of course, it was difficult for the patient to even give a non-verbal response because they were compulsively analyzing their response, but we got through the assessment more effectively, knowing they had severe OCD and set a pattern for recovery that took root.

Step 2: Develop a clear understanding of negative reinforcement
So, what was going on with this patient who clearly wanted to get better? They were stuck in a cycle of negative reinforcement. Negative reinforcement is what builds and maintains all anxiety disorders. If you fail to recognize how various thought patterns, behaviors and situations promote negative reinforcement, then you will be at great risk for being ineffective in your treatment. Negative reinforcement is the process of quick escape from something painful, such as anxiety, hunger or anger. It is the same phenomenon that happens when a toddler has a tantrum in a shop because they have been told no sweets until after dinner. The toddler starts yelling, crying and kicking. The parent fears interrupting everyone else's shopping experience and so

gives in, purchasing a cupcake. The parent tells the child, "Next time, you will have to wait until we get home." Then, the parent is surprised the next time they go to the same store and their child loudly points out the cupcakes, then cries and kicks when the parent reminds the toddler to wait until dinner before getting a cupcake. The intention of the caregiver is to teach the child to be quiet in stores and to learn patience. Even though the parent indicated that getting a cupcake was an exception to the rule, the experience for the toddler was that having a tantrum was effective. The same thing happens when parents give reassurance, allow avoidance and promote escape from triggering situations for patients with OCD.

> *Children learn that they can prevent anticipatory anxiety when they line up their negative reinforcers ahead of known triggers.*

When negative reinforcement occurs, it cements into place the situation, the thoughts, the feelings, the images and the behaviors that preceded the quick escape. It makes the child begin to believe that the only good option for handling OCD is with escape. Sadly, it also prevents the child from learning that there are other more adaptive ways of coping. It is the anxiety equivalent of giving in to a toddler's tantrum each time they demand something inappropriate. Only in this case, the inappropriate demand is for an instant reduction in anxiety. The problem with negative reinforcement is that it quickly builds anticipatory anxiety. Children learn fast that negative reinforcers work for at least a short time, and they work hard to get more negative reinforcement. They also learn they can prevent anticipatory anxiety when they line up their negative reinforcers ahead of known triggers. Let me give you an example that you might recognize.

CASE EXAMPLE

A seven-year-old child wakes up with a tummy ache and headache. There is no fever and no known family or friends who are ill, so there is no reason to suspect illness. The child complains, looks teary-eyed and says, "Pleeeeese, can I stay home from school? I feel sick. What if I really am sick?" The parent decides to keep them home from school just in case they are truly ill and the child appears to be fine as they play the rest of the day. The next morning the same thing happens and this time the child cries more and insists more loudly that they really are sick. They cry so much they gag, dry heave and refuse to eat breakfast. Even though the parent suspects there is no illness, they waver and think that perhaps one more day home might reassure the child because they recall they were complaining about some mean kids the week before. You can guess what happens next. The child worries aloud to the parent at bedtime about waking up ill and insists the parent promises no school if they again feel ill. The pattern repeats itself. Trapped between doubt and concern, the parent schedules a visit with the paediatrician, which shows them their child is in apparent good health. Then, like many of my patients, a pattern of school refusal begins that is preceded by feeling sick the night before school, crying, refusing to get out of bed, insisting that something is wrong and breaking all promises to return to school the following day.

One reason this process of negative reinforcement happens so quickly is because research shows that children born into families with a gene pool of DNA that places them at risk for anxiety disorders have the predisposition to experience single-trial learning when fearful. This means that a child whose relatives have known or suspected anxiety disorders will be at risk for developing a full set of anxiety disorder symptoms after having only one or two negative reinforcement experiences. Other children, who do not share the same anxiety-disorder-prone gene pool, may experience the same triggers and not develop symptoms of anxiety disorders. Genetic research shows that those who are at risk for an anxiety disorder may also be experiencing a more easily dysregulated response to stressors, fright and uncertainty that consists of faster and higher peaks of anxiety symptoms and a less efficient return to normalcy. For children born with the genetic tendency to develop anxiety disorders, it's like driving a race car on an off-road track that accelerates and brakes too quickly and seems overpowered for the type of road being traversed. This single-trial learning phenomenon also partly explains why it is so easy for children to relapse. Their body and brain are easily dysregulated under conditions of stress and anxiety and slow to return to normal.

Step 3: Understand how easy it is to relapse

An additional reason that children, and adults, can relapse so quickly is that the pattern of negative reinforcement that is overlearned, such as avoiding, seeking reassurance, doing mental rituals and behavioral rituals, is the thing that is easiest to do when under duress. When stressed, all people tend to do the easiest overlearned thing unless they have practiced doing a different response. Therefore, people practice fire drills and evacuation drills because they will be more likely to do the right thing when in a fear-provoking situation. The more you practice, the more likely you are to do the helpful thing when you feel scared and overwhelmed. This is why young patients with severe OCD must do lots of exposure with response prevention practice before it is reasonable to expect them to select good coping instead of negative reinforcement. The other important thing to understand, which is part of what a patient learns when they do ERP, is to inhibit the instinctive fight, flight or freeze response that makes compulsion, reassurance seeking and avoidance so compelling. Therefore, more recent iterations of ERP include random selection of exposure practices to help the patient better learn to handle the inevitable surprise situations that occur with OCD and to build self-efficacy about coping with OCD effectively. This approach is called the inhibitory learning model for treating OCD and it can give your patients an advantage in preventing relapse (Strawn *et al.*, 2021; Lebois *et al.*, 2019).

Step 4: Understand your arsenal of therapeutic interventions and people

What do you have at your disposal to help your difficult-to-treat patient besides yourself? Research shows us that we need to be willing to mix and match different interventions to best serve patients with challenging subtypes and complicated co-morbidities (Pittenger *et al.*, 2005). In my clinical practice, we don't just consider offering more intensity and duration of exposure with response prevention, we also consider medications, transcranial magnetic stimulation, supplements, nutrition, exercise, values clarification, motivational interviewing, mindfulness training and emotional self-regulation as significant interventions that may need to be added for treatment to succeed.

Step 5: Always include skills training for caregivers

We always do parent/caregiver training because their involvement is instrumental. Parents and caregivers spend more time with the patient and are often the gatekeepers for care. They need to be included in treatment to set the stage for success. Research on treatment for young people with anxiety disorders demonstrates that interventions that include caregivers improve the outcome (Wehry et al., 2015). There are also research-proven interventions for children that solely focus on working with the parents (Lebowitz et al., 2020). My recommendation is that you take advantage of this research and include caregivers in your treatment unless you have the unusual situation of a very independent and self-directed teen who lives in a home with parents who are skilled at empowering their child to manage anxiety and other difficult things.

Assume that even the most difficult parent wants the best for their child even when they express this in a way that seems intrusive, critical or disparaging.

Many therapists who work with youth choose this patient population to work with because they prefer working with younger patients and perhaps even dislike the idea of working with adults or have had negative experiences working with parents. If you have similar ideas or have felt ineffective at working with parents, I invite you to consider the following. First, understand that anxious children often have anxious parents. These parents often accidentally express their worry and anxiety with the fight component of the fight, flight or freeze response. They do this by demanding miraculous results, getting angry about scheduling, complaining about the cost of treatment or misinterpreting your suggestions or advice as criticism. Please understand they are afraid of not being able to guarantee a good life for their child. They are afraid that they have let down their child, or that their partner has let down their child, and worry that their child's need for treatment is an indictment of their parenting or a signal that their child will never have a good life. They need your compassionate response to the same degree that your identified patient needs your compassionate response. Try to do your best to assume that even the most difficult parent wants the best for their child even when they express this in a way that seems intrusive, critical or ineffective. They are no different from their child in their need for your guidance, encouragement and support. Be willing to use your clinical skills that work so well with your younger patients and forget about their adult status. My special trick for working with parents is to assume that they are accidentally promoting negative reinforcement in their children because of their own anxiety about who they think they and their children ought to be. I consider them to be my best chance for helping the identified patient because they will spend much more time with the patient and therefore have more opportunity for influence.

Toward this end, I insist that I am able to speak freely with parents and caregivers and explain to adolescent and emerging adult patients the following:

Therapist: "Science has shown that I can best help you when I am able to teach you and your parents/caregivers how to best manage your obsessions and compulsions. I do not want your parents to accidentally do things that make it harder for you to recover or that make it easier for you to get stuck with your OCD. This means that I need to be able to talk with them freely, outside our sessions, if they make mistakes or need help to improve their skills. When I do speak with them, I will let you know ahead of time, and I will tell you everything that we talk about. If your OCD has to do with embarrassing things, then we will all talk about whether that is something that you need to reveal to your parents/caregivers. Sometimes it will be better exposure and response prevention to not talk to your parents about the content of your OCD thoughts and sometimes it will be very helpful to talk to your parents about the content of your OCD thoughts. We will work on this together and make it part of your exposure practice if necessary. I know this might be different from other therapists you have worked with. I want to make this time work better for you, so that is why we are doing it this way."

I then insist that I get necessary signatures and permission from the patient, if they are old enough to give consent. This can be very important when the content of the patient's OCD concerns topics like gender identity, sexual preference, sexual assault, religious topics or confession compulsions. These topics are difficult and nuanced and parents are very likely to misunderstand the nature of the content of the obsessions or the function of the confessions. Here is an example.

CASE EXAMPLE

Ying was a 14-year-old who developed intrusive thoughts about sexually assaulting her younger siblings after she accidentally touched her brother's genital area during play wrestling and her brother yelled out, "You touched my penis!" and then told their parents. The younger brother then told several of his friends, one of whom told his mother who then texted the patient's mother that she was concerned about possible inappropriate touching. Ying then overheard her mother talking about incest and her intrusive thoughts about being a pedophile took root. Ying's mother attempted to reassure Ying by saying that it was normal for siblings to accidentally touch each other in play and to even think thoughts about their brother's or sister's genitals or even wonder about sex with a sibling. Ying was horrified by her mum's remarks and then got obsessions about having sex with her brother and sister and began avoiding all interactions with family to prevent accidental incest. Her mother tried to reassure Ying that Ying would never hurt her siblings, but Ying's OCD assumed she must be awful, as why else would she get these thoughts?

The problem in this instance is that the mother's response was well intentioned and likely to work well with the average teen who does not have OCD and who is not afraid of intrusive thoughts and needs an adult's help to normalize their experience. What Ying's mother did not understand, however, was how to handle the mushrooming and doubting nature of Ying's OCD without accidentally helping it grow. You likely have been in the same situation with patients like Ying. Learning how to respond to someone's OCD who takes fright at any comment related to the content of their OCD takes some skill building to make the conversation therapeutic. It means being able to quickly recognize the common enemy of OCD, and skipping any conversation about the content of OCD. Being able to check in early and often with Ying's parents about how to coach Ying and how to avoid well-intentioned attempts to reassure Ying early in treatment made it easier for Ying to succeed. Later, when we had her parents participate in generating spontaneous exposure triggers by making unexpected comments about the possibility of Ying being incestuous, the parents were not afraid to stand firm when Ying had a crying meltdown in response to this planned exposure that she knew would happen. The trick to success is to help the patient identify at the start that OCD is the enemy and never the content of their obsessions. Here is another similar example you might have encountered.

CASE EXAMPLE

Mohammed, a 16-year-old boy, had obsessions about the surety of his knowledge. He was an excellent student until he began high school and felt pressure to get perfect grades to get into a highly competitive university. He began to ask more questions in class and to send more emails to teachers to clarify assignments and the meaning of what he was studying. Initially, his parents and teachers thought he was being thorough, but began to worry when he was unable to finish assignments despite being told that his work and comprehension were excellent. A pattern of staying home to catch up on work, skimping on sleep to study more and requesting extra help mushroomed into compulsive slowness that affected all conversations, not just ones related to school. He was slow to finish all schoolwork, slow to respond in conversation, repeatedly asking people to repeat themselves, especially when given instructions or new information because he kept trying to verify whether he properly understood. His school gave him extended deadlines for completing work and exams because all of his marks were excellent. The end result was that he was two years behind in school with two years of incomplete classes and perfect marks. He was only able to complete work at a snail's pace so long as an adult was present to reassure him that he was indeed doing the correct thing. He was well behaved, polite, respectful and always grateful for everyone's help, which made it easy for his parents and teachers to be patient. He would preface questions with, "I don't want to be annoying, but I just want to make sure I get this right. I know this might be my OCD, but just in case it is not, would you say that again/show me again/explain that a different way?" Attempts at ERP treatment that limited him to one question or had an adult just telling him to start his homework had failed.

The dilemma for the school and parents was their difficulty in figuring out how to help this young man tolerate doubt without providing the negative reinforcement of reassurance. Discussion revealed that just having an adult present was a form of reassurance for the patient, in addition to their willingness to take on the responsibility for telling him when to write or commit to an answer. Discussion also revealed that he had an all-or-nothing quality to seeking any reassurance, such that there was no easy way to graduate his exposure practice. His previous therapists had done a reasonable thing by reducing him to only one question. For many patients, this would have worked as a method to wean him from rituals, but not for this patient. This meant that the only thing that really provoked significant anxiety was having absolutely no opportunity for getting reassurance and having no one present who even knew what it was that he had to decide and commit to in his thinking. This patient needed to feel the full effect of taking complete responsibility for his decisions instead of being allowed to do a responsibility dump to another adult he assumed had good comprehension. Trying to allow him one question was the same as allowing him to ask thousands of questions. It meant treatment was going to have to create exposure practice without any hint of reassurance and without any opportunities for dumping responsibility. It took a lot of practice and early missteps to help the school and family extricate themselves from the role of providing reassurance.

Step 6: Become expert at differential diagnosis

Properly defining the nature of the patient's OCD and co-morbid conditions is so important that I will cover it in detail in the chapter that follows. If you get this step correct, you will make treatment planning and implementation much easier. Patients with challenging subtypes of OCD often have symptoms that are difficult to detect, subtle in meaning or that seem so bizarre that they are misunderstood as psychosis. Sometimes OCD symptoms can be easily mistaken for symptoms of other conditions, such as eating disorders, autism spectrum behaviors or delusions. Patients with perfectionism focused OCD or certain types of scrupulosity may be misunderstood to be exemplars of conscientiousness, affection or politeness. The following chapter will help navigate you through the maze of separating the OCD from other disorders.

Step 7: Understand your patient's unique culture

Difficult OCD subtypes that focus on issues of faith, LGBTQ+ concerns, morality and harming are always influenced by the patient's culture of upbringing. We know that being religious does not increase the likelihood of scrupulosity OCD (Ciarrochi, 1995), but we also know that OCD hijacks the culture in which the patient resides. As mental health professionals we are all taught how to be sensitive to issues of diversity, culture and religion; however, OCD treatment often necessitates being able to grasp the nuances of specific subcultures to properly design treatment. Additionally, parents, caregivers, clergy and other support persons may need to be reassured that you can support and promote the child's subculture while simultaneously extricating the child from their OCD. For example, if the rabbi is not convinced that you will help the patient maintain a kosher lifestyle while helping the child overcome scrupulous adherence to kosher edicts, then you will lose the opportunity to help the patient. Likewise, a teen whose OCD focuses on the status of their salvation as a born-again Christian will want to see evidence of your support for their faith even though you might be agnostic or Buddhist. Similarly, an emerging adult whose OCD causes doubt about gender identity will want to know that you understand the significance of language and inclusivity before they will feel comfortable dealing with the ways their OCD plays on uncertainty and a desire to be inclusive. I have learned that often I need to go to clergy and others who are more knowledgeable and experienced than I am to help me understand the nuances I might overlook or misunderstand that can interfere with effective treatment. I also seek to find mentors in the youth's environment who are willing to understand OCD and serve as an outside conscience for guiding the patient with their moral authority. This can make it much easier to proceed in treatment when someone who has been granted moral authority by the patient and their family endorses treatment. Inevitably there will be times when this person's support and approval will make it possible for the patient to take the brave next step that you and previous mental health providers have been unable to secure.

OCD hijacks the culture in which the patient resides.

Toward this goal, I have compiled a list of questions that can guide you in finding a helpful outside moral mentor.

1. Are you familiar with OCD and exposure with response prevention therapy?

2. Have you ever counseled/advised anyone with the type of OCD that the patient experiences? If so, what has been your experience?

3. Would you be interested in learning about how I plan to treat the patient and becoming their outside guide so they can have someone they trust endorse and support their treatment? Would you be interested in learning how I see OCD affecting this patient's ability to participate fully in your community?

4. Could you explain to me what is important for me to know to help the patient participate in their faith/gender identity/ spiritual community/family? How does the average person in good standing with your community handle the thoughts and situations the patient experiences?

5. Are there any rules I need to know that are important for my patient to follow?

6. Are there any things that you believe my patient is misunderstanding or misapplying compared to the typical youth you work with?

7. Are there any types of behaviors or exposures that you/your community would consider blasphemous/inappropriate/ immoral/unwise? Are there any exceptions to this rule?

8. How do you handle uncertainty when you are unsure about something? How do you advise youth to handle their uncertainty?

Step 8: Figure out what failed in previous attempts to intervene

This step is very important. The answer will help guide you around obstacles that thwarted previous failed attempts by the family or other mental health professionals. You should be able to answer the following questions to determine the critical issues you need to address.

1. Did previous treatment accurately target exposure to all the images/thoughts/situations the patient feared?

   a. For example, if your patient tells you they have obsessions about homosexuality, do they fear the idea of being LGBTQ+ and/or do they fear not knowing for sure what their sexual preference might be? You will need to do exposure to one, the other or both feared situations, depending on the patient's OCD.

   b. Research on the treatment of OCD and other anxiety disorders shows that ERP does not generalize across obsessions and compulsions. You must treat all symptoms to remission to achieve a good long-term outcome. It's like treating cancer. You want to get rid of all of it to have the best chance of never having cancer return.

2. Did previous treatment achieve response prevention?

   a. Experience shows me that this is the single most common

reason for partial recovery from OCD. The patient was unable to sustain or even begin any significant response prevention and therefore the exposure practice was either in vain or even made OCD worse. The difficult part about response prevention is that often the challenging subtypes of OCD involve mental rituals, subtle movements or unpredictable rituals. For example, a patient might tell you that their OCD can be triggered by a random variety of situations, "If I see a number six, then I think of Satan and then whatever I am doing becomes something dedicated to Satan and I must figure out what the opposite is to do of what I was doing when I saw the six. I must pretend that I never saw the six."

3. Did the exposure and response prevention last long enough for the patient to realize they could handle it, even if their anxiety level did not drop by at least half?

4. Did treatment happen often enough that the patient and their family could sustain their home practice and not give in to the OCD? Did they get enough support from the frequency and duration of treatment?

5. Did the family know how to handle any oppositional behaviors effectively or treatment refusal effectively?

6. If the patient has not tried medication, can you persuade them to attempt medication?

    a. If the patient is already on medication, has it been adequate?

    b. Do the patient and their family see any improvement in symptoms or ability to tolerate or engage in treatment because of the medication?

    c. Do they need to get a second opinion with someone more experienced with complicated OCD?

    d. Medication has been shown to be helpful and even necessary for success with moderate to severe OCD in youth (Walter et al., 2020). When medication is effective, it can reduce the overall burden of physical anxiety, improve sleep and make it easier for the youth to think in a more helpful manner about their OCD. It will not cure OCD, but rather put a ceiling on the symptoms that makes it more manageable for the patient. My experience has been that, often, youth with difficult-to-treat OCD will need medication on an ongoing basis to better manage their OCD. This may be difficult for parents to accept, especially if they misperceive medications as being harmful.

7. Has the family or school been able to refrain from unhelpful behaviors such as providing reassurance, allowing compulsions, avoidance or accidentally promoting OCD in other ways?

   a. Has the family or school had any coaching in how to be more helpful? If not, how can you better involve them in treatment?

8. Are the patient and their family getting adequate sleep?

   a. Sleep deprivation has been known to worsen OCD (Brand & Kirov, 2011) and negate the effects of medications. Do you need to focus first on securing better sleep for everyone or make symptoms that interfere with sleep your first focus?

   b. A sleep-deprived patient and/or family has much less capacity for treatment than they might otherwise have. Kids with severe OCD often have bedtime rituals, interrupt their parents' sleep, or accidentally disrupt and delay going to bed for everyone. Unless there are life-threatening rituals that involve refusal to eat or drink, I always target sleep interfering rituals first, so it makes the rest of treatment more likely to succeed.

   c. Has the patient failed to reveal the extent of their OCD or the more embarrassing or frightening aspects of their OCD? In addition to not being able to mention the content of their OCD, patients who are digitally savvy may have done research that informed them about ERP and then gave in to the urge to avoid by keeping some, or all, of their OCD private to avoid the anticipated crucible of ERP.

Step 9: Design the ideal schedule that promotes follow through

Intensity, duration and frequency of sessions must fit the severity of the symptoms for treatment to succeed with OCD. It is a situation analogous to getting an infection that requires more than the standard first quick round of antibiotics. It might require prolonged antibiotics, special reserve use antibiotics or intravenous antibiotics to guarantee recovery. Research on treatment outcome for challenging cases of OCD demonstrates that even the most difficult and severe cases can improve or recover when duration and frequency is matched to the severity of symptoms (Endres *et al.*, 2022; Brown *et al.*, 2017). For example, some patients will respond well to weekly outpatient therapy that fits into a 45–60-minute session. Many will not. The next step would be to provide multiple sessions a week, up to six or seven days a week. Sessions may need to be lengthened to two or even three hours to accommodate the patient's ability to tolerate anxiety, to ensure response prevention or to provide an adequate amount of time for exposure to even occur. Here are some examples of how to decide the proper intensity of treatment.

- A 15-year-old girl can force herself to avoid giving in to compulsions because she saves them up for home. She has learned that she can go at least eight hours before she gives in to her compulsions. She shows the same ability to do ERP in your office by readily doing exposure and reports that she is anxious but not too much because she knows that she can "save up" her compulsions until later. Nothing you do in your office increases her anxiety beyond moderate levels and no amount of negotiating helps her stop doing compulsions once she leaves your office.

  - The ideal treatment would include sessions that happen at her home after the school day finishes during the time and place she is most likely to do rituals. She may need extended sessions and daily sessions for multiple weeks to help get her past her ability to stave off her compulsions.

- A seven-year-old boy does well in your office fighting his OCD monster, doing really anxiety-provoking exposures and refraining from compulsions until he gets home and then has prolonged crying, begging for reassurance seeking, and threatening to kill himself if the parents do not give him reassurance. He sleeps very little because he is repeatedly getting out of bed to cry and attempt to get the parents to do rituals and say reassuring things.

- Daily treatment and treatment in his home and during the time before bedtime may be especially effective for coaching the parents to refuse to provide reassurance while the boy gets used to doing exposure and response prevention. Daily treatment will give the parents the support they need and help the boy understand that he is expected to learn to cope with his anxiety without using reassurance seeking and parental rituals designed to give him quick relief. His parents likely will need coaching in implementing time out and active ignoring of tantrums and may need help rearranging where family members sleep so the patient does not ruin everyone's sleep.

- A 19-year-old tells you they can only maintain response prevention for several days between sessions and then gives in to OCD and compulsively attempts to pray for forgiveness for impure thoughts until the next session.

  - This teen will need treatment spaced so she can see her therapist at the point right before she is likely to give in to her compulsions.

- A 12-year-old tween always argues and yells at the beginning of each session for at least 30 minutes until she agrees to do exposure practice. Once she stops her anxious arguing and demands, she participates by following all instructions while grumbling and attempting to draw the therapist and parent into arguments. She has parents who find it very difficult to avoid arguing with their daughter and who frequently argue with each other about what should be done to help their daughter. You discover that these parents have never used time out, or extinction-based procedures (withholding attention, eye contact, playtime or access to desired activities in response to arguing and tantrums). They believe that it is important to get their daughter's agreement to do things that she does not want to do, despite the fact that it has never worked.

- This girl will need prolonged sessions of two or more hours so that there is ample time to wade through the initial fight/tantrum response to anxiety and to do productive multiple exposures that prove to her that she can do more than she thought possible. The parents will need role-playing practice and help to understand the value of using time out for teaching frustration tolerance and self-soothing. They will need help learning how to handle the problem at hand instead of getting distracted by arguing about technique. They will need to learn how to form an alliance to help their daughter overcome her OCD instead of getting pitted against each other.

• A 13-year-old does exposure and their anxiety level does not drop for the first 80 minutes. It takes 90 minutes of supported exposure practice for them to realize they can handle the exposure, experience success and overcome anticipatory anxiety. This happens every session.

- This patient will benefit from sessions that are three hours in length so they can see progress and learn to trust the process of exposure with response prevention. They would also benefit from daily sessions until they begin to get used to various exposure practices and experience a more rapid drop in anxiety.

• A 15-year-old with OCD and attention deficit hyperactivity disorder does five days a week of intensive exposure with response prevention practice and makes slow progress. On the weekends, he starts giving in to his compulsions despite understanding this is unhelpful. He maintains about half of his response prevention guidelines on weekdays. This has been going on for the past four weeks.

- This boy may do better in a specialized OCD partial hospitalization program or residential treatment that offers a longer window of treatment and supervised coaching around the clock to maintain response prevention.

- A 16-year-old spends every waking moment attempting to determine the right decision that glorifies God. This prevents her from getting dressed, going to school, spending time with friends and even interferes with eating and going to the bathroom. She has lost weight, fallen behind in school, and has had several urinary tract infections from not voiding her bladder enough. She has visible bruises on her knees from praying excessively. She has attempted multiple medications and several partial hospitalization programs that specialize in OCD, but with no success.

  - This teen would benefit from specialized prolonged treatment that could be found in a residential setting or a special daily outpatient program that provides prolonged twice daily two-to-three-hour sessions and daily support for response prevention.

- An eight-year-old only gets anxious and compulsive when at home because all OCD triggers occur within their home. There is nothing that you can do to make them anxious in your office, even when you have them bring into your office items associated with their OCD triggers.

  - This patient needs in home treatment and may need two or more sessions per week, depending on their caregiver's ability to follow through with home practice.

You can see from these examples that always trying to fit a patient into the typical 45–60-minutes-a-week treatment plan is likely to fail. So, the first rule for working with complicated OCD patients is to set them up for success with the frequency and duration of sessions that fits their individual profile of needs. You will need to reconfigure your schedule, your location and your length of session to fit the needs of your patient if you want them to succeed.

My formula for deciding on a treatment schedule that sets the patient up for success depends on the answers to the following questions:

1. What happens when the patient cannot do rituals? Does the patient respond in a manner that frightens or overwhelms caregivers? Do they have panic attacks? Do they run away? Do they threaten suicide? Can the caregivers handle the patient's reaction? If not, what do they need that would help them manage it better? How much support do they need from a therapist without giving up, going to the Emergency Department or getting into a battle?

2. How long can the patient and caregivers go without resorting to rituals and avoidance?

3. What time of day are the symptoms or reactions to symptoms worst? Do they need in-person help to make it through the most difficult symptoms?

4. What happens when the patient does exposure? Do they throw a tantrum? Threaten suicide? Cry? Make threats? How well do the caregivers handle the patient's response to exposure or being anxious? Do they give in easily?

5. Are there any examples of the patient or caregivers spontaneously trying exposure? Do they show signs of grit or implicit understanding and acceptance of the exposure with response prevention process? What has prevented them from doing more of this? How can you build the support they need to do more of this without your help?

6. Does the patient have the ability to tolerate other distressing emotions or frustration outside the OCD? For example, can they push themselves in sports, hobbies or music? Do they always give up easily? Do the parents always rush in to help with other upsetting situations? If they show pluck in other areas, how can you help them do this with OCD?

7. What stamina does the patient and their family have for treatment? Are they burned out and in need of more direct intervention? Can the caregivers work together or is conflict in their relationship likely to interfere with treatment? Do they lose their patience quickly and need others to do the pushing until it is less difficult for everyone?

8. Ask the patient and their family, 'How long do you think you can go between sessions while following through with home practice?'

You can see from these questions that we are trying to determine what the ideal interval is between sessions that would allow the patient and their caregivers to successfully follow through with ERP. I encourage you to ask these same questions and use your best judgment to set everyone up for success. One of the most common reasons I see patients failing in previous treatments is because they were meeting too infrequently and for too short a time even though their therapist was attempting a well-designed ERP protocol. The patient was being asked to take the right steps but without the ideal structure that kept them on track and moving forward. Having too few sessions, or sessions that are too short, is like trying to drive a thousand miles with only a five gallon can of gas for refueling your car. In this case, the refueling that needs to happen for your patient is a refueling of motivation, reminders of success, direct encouragement to do difficult things, discouragement of avoidance and compulsions, and showing them how to repeat exposures and attempt unforeseen spontaneous exposures. Caregivers may need the same refueling.

I tell patients and their caregivers that they can taper back on frequency and duration of sessions once I see that they can be diligent and strong on their own. I inform them that the sooner they develop grit about doing exposure practice and prove their OCD is no longer dictating their behavior, the sooner we can meet less frequently. Many families find this motivating and love the idea of being able to control somewhat the cost of treatment by doing their job well. I tell them that I maintain the right to judge how well the patient is following through based on how well anxiety decreases between sessions, how well they approach new exposure tasks and how well they learn to use ERP to handle spontaneous OCD triggers outside the session.

Step 10: Continually assess and redesign treatment

One question that I hear frequently from mental health professionals who are struggling with challenging OCD subtypes is, "What do I do when the patient does not seem to be making progress? Should I quit treating them?" or ,"They have tried everyone in the region and done several rounds of intensive outpatient and residential treatment. What can I possibly do to help them?" When I hear these questions, I assume that part of what is being asked is, "What is reasonable to expect from this patient? What should I be expecting from myself as a therapist? If all these other hard working and competent people had no success, then what am I likely to achieve?" Many well-intentioned therapists also secretly assume that the patient might not want to get better, or that OCD symptoms promote secondary gain, such as maintaining the family system that revolves around the patient, avoiding growing up or blocking parental expectations for academic, social or vocational achievement. My response to the first set of questions is to address the issue of accidental perfectionism, which I will cover later. My response to the issue of secondary gain is to remind the reader that OCD was believed to be untreatable when treatment focused on the meaning of symptoms. OCD did not become treatable until treatment focused on dismantling negative reinforcers. Thus, it is safe to assume that when someone is struggling, the system of negative reinforcement has not been accurately described or addressed.

The issue of accidental therapist perfectionism, or creating an overly narrow definition of expectations for the patient and family, is a common problem for many therapists when working with diffi-cult-to-treat subtypes. My experience has shown me that it may take quite a bit longer to hit the same milestones in treatment as it does with subtypes that are easier to treat. If you conclude too quickly that the patient is not making progress, then you risk premature cessation of treatment. My standard for continuing treatment is to see any improvement, no matter how slight, as significant improvement. Since many of the difficult-to-treat subtypes involve perspective taking and inferential thinking, the intellectual and academic development of the child becomes relevant in a way that does not apply to contamination, symmetry, certain types of checking or ordering rituals or cleaning compulsions. Additionally, willingness to become independent in taking perspective and making moral choices may not fully develop until the child is in their late teens or early twenties. These factors can slow down the patient's willingness and ability to express, understand or attempt certain types of exposure tasks or to maintain response prevention. Consider the example of Roger, which illustrates what happens when a patient is not able to properly describe the nature of his obsessions.

CASE EXAMPLE

Roger's OCD began in kindergarten when he began occasionally getting upset with his friends if they messed up his toys. He would have a tantrum and insist that the other boy had ruined his toy when there was no sign of chips, dents or scratches. His family responded by hiding preferred toys when he had playdates and reassuring him that his toys were still in mint condition. Several years later he came home from school crying about how his markers and pencils were ruined and began keeping his pencils and markers on his person to prevent others from using them. He would cry if others touched his backpack or school materials, and he threw away any school supplies he deemed ruined, even if they were brand new. He was diagnosed with OCD contamination subtype. He completed a short course of partially successful ERP and continued to have occasional crying episodes about his personal belongings being ruined. At age 12, he got his first mobile phone and began worrying about whether it was still in good condition, and started to compulsively clear all data and reset the phone every night. The same problem occurred when he began using a digital tablet and laptop, which meant he would often lose homework, contacts and important messages.

When he re-entered treatment, he explained his obsession as being about keeping his important belongings pristine, like they were before he first used them. He cried as he explained that he was tortured by the idea that things had to be used up. When asked if this was a new obsession, he reported that he had always felt this way, though he had never been able to properly describe his obsession until recently.

Instead of using the idea of contamination for ERP, I focused on exposure to thoughts about the impermanence of all things, along with response prevention to attempt to keep things pristine. Then he made real headway in treatment.

When you pay attention to how you assess your patient, how you time treatment sessions, when you involve all the significant caregivers and determine what likely went wrong with any previous treatment attempts, then you can set the stage for successful treatment. Too many therapists make the mistake of designing a great treatment plan that works and then accidentally continue to follow the initial plan even though it no longer works for the patient. Making the effort to be flexibly thorough will pay dividends when you enter the active phase of treatment. Next, we will learn how to best assess the patient's symptoms so you can be confident you are creating a relevant and effective range of exposure tasks and response prevention guidelines for challenging subtypes of OCD.

If you would like to view a demonstration of how to implement some of the strategies mentioned in this chapter, please go to https://library.jkp.com/redeem using the code ZVEAZDD.

CHAPTER 2

Differential Diagnosis and Setting Up Exposure with Response Prevention Practice

Teasing apart OCD from generalized anxiety disorder (GAD), specific phobias, autism spectrum disorders and other co-morbid conditions can pose some challenges. Research shows us that 70 percent of youth with OCD have one or more co-morbid conditions (Sharma *et al.*, 2021). Other anxiety disorders are the most likely co-morbid condition, followed by depression and attention deficit hyperactivity disorder (ADHD). When OCD is not successfully treated, the risk for co-morbid depression increases to 70 percent or more (Fineberg *et al.*, 2020). Although it is true that exposure-based treatments are best for all anxiety disorders, including unified treatment protocols that are applied regardless of diagnosis (Barlow *et al.*, 2017), there are nuances of treatment for each disorder that influence effective treatment. This is especially true when it involves a complicated subtype of OCD. For example, a patient who fears getting sick with cancer might meet criteria for either OCD, GAD, post-traumatic stress disorder (PTSD), specific phobia or illness anxiety disorder. Let me explain.

If the patient has OCD about illness, they typically will recognize, at least during the onset of their OCD, that their fear of cancer was unmerited. They might get obsessions about catching cancer from being near someone who had cancer or walking near a facility that treats cancer. They might have to do decontamination compulsions even though they know cancer is not transmissible. They might fear thinking about cancer, because their OCD tells them that if they think about cancer, then they will have cancer. Clearly, magical intrusive thoughts caused by thought-action fusion (Shafran & Rachman, 2004) might be the problem. Thought-action fusion is typical of OCD and occurs when someone believes that thinking about something will make it real or make it happen. For example, a patient might get an intrusive thought about dying of cancer and then feel as though they will now get cancer because they thought about cancer. Some might call this magical thinking, the kind that young children have when they fear the picture they drew of a monster will release a monster during the night. Thought-action fusion is like this but is not tied to developmental or intellectual age. Thought-action fusion can drive patients to focus on avoiding intrusive thoughts for fear the presence of the thought just increased the odds of the thought coming true. Additionally, someone with OCD will almost always have multiple subtypes of OCD, either at the same time or over the course of time. This is not true of the other anxiety disorders, except GAD, in which worries can appear in multiple contexts and vary over time.

A patient who has GAD about getting cancer might have had a grandparent who died of cancer and overheard their parents talking about familial and lifestyle risks for cancer. They might worry about avoiding foods and pollution and do a lot of researching about healthy lifestyle and lowering risk for cancer. They might ask lots of questions about whether they might someday die of cancer. They might also worry about other things, such as grades, being late, getting enough sleep, their family finances, or the quality of their friendships. They will typically have other physical symptoms of anxiety, such as insomnia, headaches, upset stomach or muscle aches. Worry also makes sense to the worrier and youth, who feels as though their worry is merited, unlike those who experience intrusive unwanted thoughts caused by OCD. The worry that appears to be like OCD is typically one of many worries the patient has experienced.

A youth with PTSD which manifests as anxiety about illness might have had a close friend or parent who died of cancer. They might have intrusive thoughts about the death of the person who died. They might be worried about dying of cancer or about others dying of cancer and do checking for symptoms and reassurance seeking about what will happen in the future with regards to sudden death by cancer. Their goal in checking is to establish safety and to ward off the possibility of a similar traumatic event from recurring. Nightmares might cause them to forestall going to sleep for fear of experiencing another nightmare. They might avoid all mention of cancer-related things, have body aches and poor appetite. Their preference will be to never think about or recall their past traumatic experience and to avoid any situation that might trigger recall or symptoms related to PTSD. They might show lots of irritability and prefer to self-isolate rather than do activities they once enjoyed. Like someone with OCD, they will tell you that they do not want to think about their intrusive thoughts, and they feel compelled to do compulsive things to avoid thinking about past traumatic memories. Unlike OCD, they have a constant reference point of the past traumatic experience that guides their decisions to avoid, ward off or keep quiet about their recall of the past. Their symptoms will revolve around this goal.

Specific phobia might manifest as a circumscribed fear of cancer, and other serious illnesses, because the young person fears they might need treatments involving needles. They avoid being near places that might have ill people. They might avoid looking at, hearing about or seeing anything that reminds them of cancer treatment, intravenous therapy or blood collection campaigns. They might get really upset when they hear about a fundraising walk to support a cancer-related cause. They will be terrified of getting vaccinations, blood tests or skin pricks and may not have completed their scheduled vaccinations due to intense fear. Unlike OCD, their symptoms stem from a desire to avoid needles and injections, and do not extend to other areas. Their fears are always triggered by any reminder of needles, no matter how loose the association, and they believe their attempts at avoidance make sense even though they can recognize that their phobia is out of proportion compared to others. Those who have OCD are highly likely to have multiple subtypes of OCD, both simultaneously and over time. Specific phobias do not change once they emerge and focus on one specific trigger.

Lastly, illness anxiety disorder is a category in which the person worries about getting seriously ill or dying, but otherwise has no other disorders that explain this worry. Their worry is triggered by real physical symptoms that are misinterpreted as potential signs of serious illness. It is the equivalent of having worry, but only about illness and dying. Reassurance seeking and avoidance are done for the purpose of determining whether the person has a serious illness or to avoid learning that they do. They may have worries and intrusive thoughts about cancer, dying and death. They might avoid all mention of cancer and terminal illness, and avoid situations that remind them of cancer, dying or death. They may even do special ritualistic behaviors to help ward off cancer, dying and death, such as praying compulsively, knocking on wood or other superstitious actions. A patient with illness anxiety disorder may also have a chronic or serious illness, but their anxiety, reassurance seeking and avoidance interfere with their ability to live and enjoy the present moment because they are misinterpreting their current health status. Additionally, they have worry-supporting beliefs that highlight the tragedy of serious illness and death when compared to their non-anxious peers.

So, you can see how a similar set of symptoms can take on a different diagnostic flavor, depending on the patient's perception of the problem, the purpose of their response to anxiety triggers and the nature of the trigger. No wonder it can be so confusing to figure out what to target and how to treat patients with OCD, especially when they have co-morbid conditions and poor insight into their symptoms. It is incumbent on you, the therapist, to tease apart the tangle of symptoms by asking careful questions and refraining from making assumptions too quickly because a behavior appears to be compulsive, or a thought appears to be intrusive. It means that one of the most important questions you can ask while getting to know your patient is, "How come they are doing this? Thinking this? Avoiding this? What do they hope to gain by thinking and acting this way?" You need to be able to answer this question with more detail than "avoiding feeling anxious" and not mistakenly assume that there is secondary gain when making a differential diagnosis. I always want to be able to explain to myself what thoughts, beliefs and assumptions make this patient think and act the way they do. Then I can better fit the exposure with response prevention practice to the patient.

What is unique about OCD?

OCD has several qualities that are unique. All anxiety disorders can result in avoidance, panic attacks, intrusive or unwanted thoughts, seemingly ritualistic behaviors, reassurance seeking and oppositional behaviors, so the presence of these behaviors is not a sure sign of OCD. It is helpful to review what is unique about OCD to enable you to clarify the diagnosis and the various facets of your patient's OCD and other likely diagnoses. Some symptoms are common to many pediatric mental health disorders, such as panic attacks, oppositional behaviors and reassurance seeking. The presence of panic attacks is a marker of severity for any anxiety disorder and a risk factor for suicidality (Baillie & Rapee, 2005). Oppositional behaviors are an indication of the child's personality, family pattern of emotional expression, emotion regulation and parenting style. The same is true for reassurance seeking. These symptoms identify markers for treatment, such as parenting skills, tantrum management, self-regulation skills and over-parenting. They also need to be incorporated into the exposure plan, which will be reviewed in the following chapters.

Hallmarks of OCD

Obsessions are experienced as ego dystonic, at least at the beginning of the disorder. This means that the patient realizes there is something that does not make sense, or is otherwise not a product of their own wishes, desires or self. The obsession has a foreign and not right quality about it that is different from worry. Worry makes sense to the worrier because it is understood to be a helpful way to manage uncertainty by focusing on and preparing for the worst-case scenario. Obsessions, on the other hand, appear to just crop up without any warning or rational explanation that makes sense to the patient. Obsessions are the mental equivalent of accidentally opening spam in your email, whereas worries are the mental equivalent of believing you should open your spam because it might have an important message.

Overvalued ideation

Another significant difference is that OCD compulsions or rituals are done *just in case the obsession might come true*, even though the patient knows that this is highly unlikely or impossible. This is called overvalued ideation. Overvalued ideation is the fear that obsessions might be true, even though the patient initially recognizes the obsessions are untrue.

The one exception to this rule is when very young patients who still believe in magical thinking also have OCD. They may lack insight but engage in rituals to reduce anxiety just as older patients might. Patients with overvalued ideation may come to believe that what they obsess about and how they handle it with compulsions and avoidance is reasonable. They may even demand that others follow their wishes. Typically, when this occurs it is when someone has had a long and severe course of OCD and they are desperately attempting to avoid the thing they fear. I will discuss how to manage overvalued ideation in later chapters.

Patients with overvalued ideation often clearly recognize their obsessions and compulsions are ridiculous but go ahead just to make sure they are okay or to make a desperate attempt to avoid getting stuck in their OCD. For example, a teen told me, "I know I made a commitment to Christ and I am supposed to be saved, but what if I accidentally denied Christ without meaning to? What if I made a pact with the Devil?"

Patients may dread their compulsions more than their obsessions

Some patients with OCD will be more afraid of worsening their OCD symptoms than they fear the content of their OCD. They may have excellent insight but dread the aftermath of getting stuck in lengthy compulsions. They will fear rocking the boat of their OCD because they dread having to do more compulsions. They may fear obsessions, but what they fear most is doing anything that triggers or prolongs the resultant compulsions. For example, an 11-year-old avoids touching anything a sibling touched for fear she might get her imaginary friend sick, but what makes it most difficult for her to face triggers to her OCD is her fear of having to avoid everything in the house, including food, drinking water, and even sleeping so she can monitor whether or not she touches anything.

OCD is never logical and the content of obsessions may not be the problem

OCD is never logical even though it might seem to have a symbolic or interpersonal pattern. There is always an absurd quality to OCD. Many parents and therapists get confused by this and accidentally assume use of logic will be helpful. My experience shows me that even though the patient may have a certain logic to justify their desire to give in to their OCD, in the end, the goal is always to guarantee certainty and safety from OCD triggers, even when it can be easily refuted as being a useless or silly thought or action. OCD can always up the ante by using doubt, "What if this time it really happens?!" Additionally, OCD has a capricious quality, one in which the obsession can continually shift as soon as the patient feels comfortable. For example, I often see children who say, "My OCD always tells me that if I think about my OCD then the next thing I do is bad even if it is something good," or, "I never know what my OCD will say. If I move left then someone will die and then when I move right it tells me someone will die." If you keep this in mind, you will avoid the temptation to create an overly simplistic framework for intervention. Let me give you an example.

CASE EXAMPLE

Sanjay was a teen with scrupulosity OCD. He feared going to Hell, even though he was not religious and had not been raised in a Christian family. He felt tortured by the realization that his OCD controlled him, even though he did not believe in life after death. He felt constantly distracted due to intrusive thoughts, such as, "You will spend eternity burning in Hellfire!" He even began praying and attending a local church to try and rid himself of his OCD.

His previous therapists had instructed him to imagine being in Hell and repeating phrases such as, "I am going to Hell. There is nothing I can do to escape Hell." They had him stop all research about Christianity, stop praying and stop attending church. Despite following these guidelines, he got worse. He began medication, but this failed to offer much improvement.

Since both Sanjay and his therapist verified that he had done ERP properly, I knew the assigned tasks must not have hit the exposure target. So, I asked, "What belief, assumption or attitude would make these symptoms so terrible for this patient if it is not about going to Hell?" Since he said that he did not believe in any of the intrusive thoughts he experienced, I knew that there was something about having intrusive thoughts that bothered him more than the content of his thoughts. I asked him about this, and his response confirmed that what he most hated was having to think about things that were foreign to his values, sense of productivity and integrity. His real fear turned out to be having uncontrolled thoughts that made no sense to him. He would have had a similar reaction to other intrusive thoughts that seemed nonsensical or useless.

Subsequently, we focused his exposure on the idea of having permanently uncontrolled thoughts, always being cluttered with useless ideas and never being able to focus on meaningful things. We had him deliberately think about other things he considered useless, like researching how many celebrities whitened their teeth or the estimated number of potholes in his city. We made him repeat the phrase, "I will never be rid of my obsessions, and I will never be able to think about anything worthwhile without OCD ruining it. I will go insane from useless thoughts." He was finally able to make progress in treatment.

OCD takes the same form in children as in adults

OCD is also unusual because it takes the same form in young children as it does in adults. There is no pediatric version of OCD because the same obsessions and compulsions can occur across the lifespan. If you are used to assessing young children using the speech and content patterns typical of a young child, using play therapy or observation, then you might fail to detect obsessions and intrusive thoughts that contain what is traditionally understood as adult content. For example, I have seen kindergarteners who have explicit sexual obsessions or violent harming obsessions that bely their lack of exposure to adult media. Children who are prepubescent may develop intrusive thoughts about pedophilia, raping parents or pets. An eight-year-old might have disturbing thoughts about whether he is real, truly human, or in the same reality as others. You need to be able to inquire about sensitive content in a manner that is calm, conveys no judgment and shows that you are an old hand at hearing such stuff. Below is my best strategy for handling delicate content areas.

Interviewing younger children about delicate OCD content

1. Explain that OCD can be really naughty and scary because it can make children think embarrassing or scary thoughts they never thought of before.

2. Tell them about other children's intrusive thoughts using age-appropriate language, for example, "I worked with a girl your age whose OCD kept making her think about touching her cat's private parts," or, "I worked with a boy your age who kept thinking about poking people's eyes or bottoms with pencils." Try to cover a large array of sexual, violent or horrific thoughts that might mimic the patient's intrusive thoughts.

3. Ask them if they have ever had any thoughts like any of these children and observe their response carefully, looking for widened eyes, tears or flinching.

4. If the child shows agreement or a behavioral response that suggests you got close to the content of their intrusive thoughts, acknowledge their distress and suggest that OCD sometimes likes to scare children even more by telling them that if they talk about the thoughts, then they might come true or it might mean they are a bad child. For example, "Has your OCD ever scared you this way? Did you know that this is a big fat lie because nothing OCD says is ever true?" (You are trying to set the stage for helping the patient learn to ignore the content of their OCD.)

When a patient is adolescent or an emerging adult, the same phenomenon can occur, only fear of humiliation or being misunderstood as dangerous or insane can become the barrier that prevents disclosing intrusive thoughts of a sexual, violent or painful nature. When this happens, you can give explicit examples of patients who have horrific, harming, LGBTQ+, sexual or blasphemous obsessions and inquire if this sort of thought has invaded their consciousness. It is important to mention the most graphic thoughts so you can normalize the content of the patient's intrusive thoughts and perhaps even exceed the disturbing nature of their thoughts. This helps lower the barrier to disclosure. If you are successful, patients will often look wide-eyed, startled, or teary-eyed with relief to know they are not alone. I also do not ask the patient to fully disclose the content of their thoughts at this point, until I help establish hope for recovery. The next step is very important because it often unlocks the patient's willingness to disclose the content of their intrusive thoughts. The best way to help create hope is to describe how others overcame their similar obsessions. You can do this by saying something like this:

Therapist: "I don't know if this is what your OCD keeps saying in your mind, but I have seen a lot of kids like you who used to get thoughts they hated about things to do with sex, hurting other people like stabbing them with a pencil or the knife from the kitchen, murdering their grandparents or pets, pushing people out the window or in front of a car or doing things that have to do with sex with their friends, family or teachers. I have met some kids who get thoughts about wanting to be with the Devil or doing something bad against God. You know what is so cool? They all discovered that it was just OCD bothering them and they could get better by doing the practice I am going to teach you. Have you had any thoughts like these?"

Narrowing down the content of unmentionable intrusive thoughts

After normalizing the patient's intrusive thoughts and describing how others who are similar have succeeded, I find that many patients are willing to begin either disclosing the content of their intrusive thoughts or verifying the type of intrusive thought, such as sexual, violent or horrific. If they continue to struggle to indicate the type of intrusive thought, you can use multiple choice to determine what about their thoughts makes it difficult for them to disclose. You could say something like this:

Therapist: "It looks as if your OCD does not want you to mention this. Could you tell me which letter matches what your

OCD is making you think? A is 'If I talk about it, it will come true.' B is 'If I tell you about it, you will be shocked and think I am dangerous or insane.' C is 'If I say it aloud, it means that I really am a bad person.'"

Then you can directly address the patient's fears about the meaning of their intrusive thoughts by reviewing the nature of OCD, the difference between people with OCD and those who commit horrific or inappropriate acts. You also discuss the nature of thought-action fusion beliefs in OCD. Thought-action fusion is the belief that thinking something increases the likelihood of that thing coming true. People with OCD are much more likely to have thought-action fusion than those without. It explains how people with OCD can become so fearful of intrusive thoughts becoming true, even when they logically realize this is not the case (Shafran & Rachman, 2004).

Thought-action fusion is the belief that thinking something increases the likelihood of that thing becoming true. People with OCD are much more likely to have thought-action fusion than those without.

I have found that using this multiple-choice method without requiring the patient to give details helps me focus in on the nature of the intrusive thoughts more quickly than just waiting for the patient to get comfortable volunteering information. I also believe that it is helpful to hear someone comfortably talk about graphic, disturbing thoughts in a matter-of-fact way as if it is no big deal. I have had some teens and children tell me the reason they could talk to me was because I was not trying to be reassuring, like their parents or a previous therapist. They misinterpreted the therapist's or parents' overly active attempt to make them feel comfortable as being patronizing and alarming. Why else would they make such a fuss about it not being a big deal? If you think about it, how does it come across to you when someone is accidentally overly dramatic in trying to be kind? It feels icky and as if they feel sorry for you. No patient wants that experience.

Cognitive self-consciousness

One area that research shows is uniquely affected in OCD is thinking about thinking. This is called cognitive self-consciousness (Tümkaya et al., 2018). Patients with OCD have a higher level of cognitive self-consciousness than those with other anxiety disorders. This shows up in the more difficult-to-treat subtypes in which patients report lots of thinking, rumination and analyzing of the meaning of their obsessions and mental compulsions. This thinking about thinking is experienced as being unpleasant but feels important and significant to the patient because they misperceive it as a method to gain clarity of thought. It has a circular quality that always ends up back at the starting point of feeling uncertain. Many patients with difficult-to-treat subtypes of OCD will feel compelled to clearly understand what it is they thought, what it means that they had a thought and what the future implications of their thinking might be. When this occurs, it can be tricky and tedious to get a clear picture of mental compulsions. For example, a patient might say, "I am okay with being gay or bi(sexual), but I am not sure I am gay or bi. I get thoughts about guys and I get thoughts about girls and then I am not sure what it means. I try to decide how I feel each time I think about girls or guys or what happens in my groin when I think about them. Then I am not sure if I was paying proper attention to what I was thinking or maybe I was just imagining it. What if I made it happen just because I have OCD?"

Staying on track with assessment

Patients with more difficult-to-treat subtypes can be challenging to assess because their mental rituals, rumination and recurring intrusive thoughts interfere with reporting symptoms. It can feel like my springer spaniel's typical chase after birds; she used to run out the door to chase the bird she saw through the window, then sharply veer off to chase another bird that was closer, and finally veer off toward the first bird because she saw it flying away. Patients may have a difficult time describing what goes on inside their minds, especially if the rituals are mental, involve trying to obtain a "just right" feeling or more abstract concepts such as perfection, maintaining pristine quality, completion or a special quality that matches a symbol. The capricious oscillating quality of their OCD might make it impossible to explain the "rules" or reasons for doing compulsions. They might also have no specific feared consequence other than the possibility of getting intrusive thoughts. For example, I have had many patients tell me that they have intrusive thoughts about something bad happening, but no actual idea of what the bad thing might be. Some patients might have to do mental rituals until they obtain a feeling of completeness, perfection or things being round. They might have to create a feeling of balance or goodness or must mentally categorize everything according to changing rules. They might seem hesitant to describe these rituals because they are difficult to define and describe, leading the therapist to mistakenly conclude the patient is avoiding mentioning a feared consequence of failing to do compulsions. The best way to address assessing the presence of these obscure facets of OCD is to use structured assessment tools that keep you on track even when your patient's OCD flits about and is difficult to describe.

I recommend using the child version of the Yale-Brown Obsessive Compulsive Scale (Y-BOCS). The Y-BOCS is free and in the public domain (see the Resources section at the back of the book). It helps you to assess the wide variety of subtypes in OCD while giving you clinically sensitive severity ratings. I like using the Y-BOCS because it helps set the stage for designing exposure with response prevention therapy and allows me to quickly assess progress that is clinically meaningful. Structured clinical interviews are also useful to prevent sloppiness in your assessment of co-morbid conditions. They use standard criteria from the *Diagnostic and Statistical Manual of Mental Disorders, Fifth Edition* (*DSM-V*) (American Psychiatric Association, 2022) for diagnosis in a format that is friendly for both the therapist and the patient. Research shows that the more time you spend on assessment, the more likely you are to get it right (Ramirez Basco *et al.*, 2000). Sadly, clinicians across specialties have been shown to get sloppier as they get more competent because they falsely believe they are getting more skilled (Ericsson, Krampe & Tesch-Römer, 1993; Duckworth *et al.*, 2011)! You can find a list of clinical structured interviews in the Resources section at the end of this book. If you are not already following a system of structured clinical interview, I suggest you try it out.

Additionally, I like to use a structured clinical interview for assessing for the presence of other anxiety disorders and likely co-morbid conditions that commonly occur with OCD. I prefer the Anxiety Disorders Interview Schedule for the *DSM-V* (listed in the Resources section at the end of this book) because it has both a child and parent version. The parent version is especially useful when a patient is very young. Family members and caregivers tend to be the expert on what is observable, and patients are the ones who best know what happens inside their mind.

Assessing obsessive slowness and/or obsessive doubt

Another challenge for assessing youth with OCD is what to do when your patient has obsessive slowness or obsessive doubt and therefore cannot give succinct or useful answers during your assessment. This can be agonizing for everyone. My suggestion in this situation is to rely on family, caregivers, school staff and previous mental health professionals to get as much information as possible. You will also have to be willing to design and start treatment even though you might feel uncertain about what the patient fears because they are unable to adequately express or describe their experience of OCD. Typically, patients with obsessive slowness or obsessive doubt will repeat, correct and endlessly edit what they say in response to your questions. I suggest handling this situation by first verifying if the patient is doubting what they say and think or if they are getting stuck finding the perfectly correct words. Once I verify with the patient which is occurring, I say something like this:

Therapist: "This must be really frustrating to have your OCD make you feel so unsure about everything you think and say. The good news is that we are going to do our best to help you learn how to better manage your OCD and we can do that by knowing something about it without having to perfectly know everything. I may have to cut you off once I think I get the basic idea of what you are saying so we can learn about your other symptoms. We can always come back around to it later, but for now it is more important for me to get a big picture of your OCD even if I do not get all the details."

Then I ask caregivers or parents to give me information so I can obtain a better approximation of what the patient intends to say. "Your mum says that you always want to be sure you say the right thing and that you keep checking in your mind to make sure you get the words right. Is this true?" I try to give the patient some yes/no type questions that do not demand as much thought and effort compared to the typical open-ended therapist's query. For example, "Does your OCD insist you find the perfect wording?" or, "Does your OCD make you very slow because you have to be certain of what you are thinking?"

When the patient's OCD prevents them from speaking

You may encounter situations in which the patient's OCD prevents them from speaking or indicating in any way what the nature of their OCD might be. For example, some patients might have obsessions or compulsions that prevent them from speaking, moving or doing any volitional behaviors. Their OCD might have scrupulous rules about perfectly aligning their intentions with God or making sure that anything they do reflects a sincere intention to do no harm and does not allow them to move unless they can be certain they are pure in thought and behavior. They may have obsessions about not moving, not speaking, or simply holding a certain position. For example, one patient I met had been misdiagnosed as being psychotic and catatonic because he stood in the corner of his room without responding until he fell asleep and collapsed. He was trying to complete a prayer ritual, praying without ceasing. His compulsion was to attempt to stand still and focus on God without making any movement or without deviating from paying attention to God, and this prevented him from responding to anyone else. The more people tried to interrupt him, the more he tried to stand still and focus on God, hoping to finally get the ritual right and therefore to complete his compulsion. I have met other patients who could not speak because they feared saying a curse word, blaspheming God, or doing something without first clearing their mind of bad thoughts. In these instances, it is important to remember that disorders such as schizophrenia and catatonia are rare compared to OCD and that these other disorders are more prevalent in families without OCD and other anxiety disorders.

The unwilling patient

Lastly, you may encounter the situation in which a patient is able to talk about their symptoms but is unwilling to cooperate with assessment because they have no interest in treatment. This situation usually arises when a patient's OCD symptoms and/or oppositional behaviors have become so extreme and disruptive that others are insisting on treatment without the patient's consent. The next chapter will teach you how to handle oppositional behaviors, including refusal to cooperate with an assessment. My experience with these kinds of patients is that they are simply scared and have had the unfortunate experience of learning that yelling, fighting, arguing, threatening suicide, threatening to run away, and creating an uproar works to avoid anxiety in their setting. Remembering to reframe the meaning of their behavior is helpful to keep you in your compassionate, gentle but strong zone so you do not give up and accidentally believe they cannot be helped until they cooperate. My experience with patients who are stuck in the fight mode of fight, flight or freeze is they can become wonderful energetic patients who are extremely grateful someone did not give up on helping them escape the prison of their OCD. They just needed someone who was not intimidated or fooled by their dramatic way of showing their fear. Here are some helpful reframes to help you keep up your courage and compassion in the face of opposition:

When the patient says...	Helpful reframe
You can't make me. I have my rights!	They are just scared and do not yet believe they can overcome their OCD. As long as they depend on someone to feed, clothe and shelter them, we have leverage against their OCD
If you make me do that, I will kill myself!	They are so lost in their OCD they cannot imagine doing any exposure or response prevention. Most kids and adults with severe anxiety disorders have moments of feeling as if they would rather die than experience another moment of fear. That is not wanting to die. It's just wanting to avoid fear
I won't go to school/get in the car/get out of bed. I am never coming to this office again!	They are really scared and do not yet understand they can learn step by step how to face their fears. We can bring therapy to them if they cannot come to us

I will never talk to you again! You are a ****! You just do this for money and to torture kids like me!	They are just really frightened and afraid they cannot make progress. Given what they are saying, it might be nice to have them keep their thoughts to themselves. We just need to help them learn they can succeed against OCD

Getting important information about the patient's context

You need to learn more than just which symptoms and diagnostic categories fit the patient. You also need to thoroughly assess the patient's home and school environments for how they help or hinder in overcoming OCD. Two important areas should be addressed, over-accommodation and how oppositional behaviors are addressed. You are probably well aware that over-accommodation—the clinician's term for helicopter parenting (over-involved hovering parenting that too quickly intervenes before the child can learn how to manage anxiety and distress) and snowplow parenting (extreme over-involvement in which parents literally pave the way for the child such as doing their homework or chores and handling all of the child's problems and mistakes)—is a significant risk factor for children developing anxiety disorders, depression, suicidality and substance abuse (O'Connor et al., 2020). It is critically important that you treat parents and caregivers and advise school staff who accidentally offer over-accommodation. Untreated over-accommodation will impede progress and prevent full recovery, even when the patient is motivated to be more independent. Failing to teach significant adults how to stop referring the child to the Emergency Department or crisis hotline or giving in each time they get oppositional due to anxiety will have the same deleterious effect.

When assessing over-accommodation, you should ask the following questions of any adults who are caring for the patient. The answers to these questions will help identify which parenting beliefs and skills you should address. If you think you need a refresher in the role that accommodation plays in OCD, read the article by Monzani et al. (2020).

Questions to ask caregivers

1. What do you do when your child is having a rough moment with their OCD? What do you say? What do you think? How do you act?

2. When your child is frustrated and wants to give up on something, what do you say and do?

3. When your child cannot figure out how to do their schoolwork, what do you do? Do you make them talk to the teacher? Do you try to help them? Do you ever do the problem or essay for them, or read their schoolwork so you can help them?

4. Have you ever called your child in sick because they stayed up too late, slept poorly or just did not want to go in to school that day?

5. When your child is crying, what do you do?

6. When your child expresses anger or frustration with you, what do you do?

7. When your child says they do not love you, how do you feel and what do you do?

8. Do you like to watch your child at sports, music, arts or theatre practice? Do you think it is wise to drop them off and only watch the match, game or final production?

9. What do you do when your child comes home from school and is crying about a teacher or peer, or complaining about being mistreated?

10. When you believe your child is bullied, what do you do? Do you help them solve the problem or do you talk to the school, coach, and so on?

11. Do you think your child has ever lied to you or done something that you seriously disapprove of? (Most parents who believe they have a very close attached relationship falsely assume their child does not lie to them. They are wrong! I frequently hear patients say, "Don't let my mum or dad know, but they think I

would never…and I do. I just don't want to hurt their feelings. They couldn't handle it.")

12. What do you do when your child misbehaves or breaks the rules? Do you have consequences? Do you talk to them? When you talk to them, what do you say or do? Most over-accommodating parents are focused on having a peaceful and loving relationship with their child and avoid conflict, even when it is necessary. They prefer to have conversations that result in hugs and kisses versus taking a strong stance on the child managing a mistake or problem. When this occurs, patients learn that good intentions are more important than good behavior and they feel little motivation to gain coping skills. Children also learn they can avoid consequences when they say the right things, which promotes entitlement and fear of risk taking.

13. What do you think when your child shows their OCD symptoms or is in emotional pain? Over-accommodating parents often view their child's suffering as a tragedy that might create trauma as opposed to a normal variation on the human experience of suffering. Healthy parents feel sadness when they see their child suffer but can focus on helping their child cope because they know this is what matters most for the child's future. They realize that feeling loved does not confer skill in fighting OCD. They know that only exposure practice will confer skill, regardless of affection between the child and their parent.

When I identify over-accommodation, I insist the parents and caregivers participate in treatment so they learn how to become an effective OCD coach for their child. I act as a role model for how to coach the patient. I have parents take turns coaching their child to do exposure tasks after I show them how to do it. I give live feedback and involve the patient in giving live feedback to their parent during the session and between sessions. Usually, in any type of therapy the focus is on what is wrong with the patient, as opposed to what needs to be changed by the parents. I find that patients enjoy giving corrective feedback, even when they are oppositional. I have also discovered that patients are unusually perceptive and accurate in their feedback, even when they have the opportunity to extract some revenge by giving failing marks. My goal is for the parent to develop insight into the negative effect of their over-accommodation and become motivated to avoid stepping into the over-accommodation trap. I do this by following a series of steps, detailed below.

Working with parents

Step 1: Have the patient pretend to be the parent while the therapist pretends to be the patient during an example of difficult OCD symptoms. Ask the patient to show what the parent does when they have their OCD symptoms. Tell them to give you the unvarnished truth and to be as much like their parent/caregiver as possible. Then after you have seen what the parent does, ask the parent to be the patient and you pretend to be the parent. Tell the parent that you are going to do the role play twice and the patient gets to be the director to let each of you know if you are doing your part right. On the first role play, act like the parent as portrayed by the patient. Then repeat the role play by acting the part of a parent who is calm when confronted with OCD, who does not hover, instruct, worry, seek reassurance or blow up with anxiety about the patient's rituals. In other words, act the way you do when you work with patients. Then ask the parent, "Which way was more helpful? What made the second one work better for you? Which one made it easier to deal with the situation?" Then ask the patient to explain how they feel the same way when their parent is in anxious over-accommodation mode. This exercise usually creates a significant and heartfelt "Aha!" moment for the parent/caregiver that works much better than a therapist's well-meant explanation of the science behind the rationale for giving up over-accommodation.

Step 2: Have the patient report back on how well the parent/caregiver avoided reminding them to do OCD practice, schoolwork or other things the child should be doing by themselves, avoided asking them how they were feeling with respect to their OCD (this is usually a symptom of a worried parent seeking reassurance) or avoided nagging them to do something the patient failed to do. The goal is to decrease parental hovering, reassurance seeking and nagging so the patient learns to manage their OCD in an age-appropriate manner. Have the patient give a grade such as they would get in school. Parents love earning their child's approval just as much as children love earning their parents' approval. This grade report system helps motivate parents and caregivers to keep practicing because there is accountability and deserved approval when the parent decreases over-accommodation.

Step 3: This exercise works best for pre-teens and older patients. Set up the "Nag Rule" which states the parent/caregiver must immediately pay a fine for any infraction of the "No nagging about treatment, recovery, home practice, schoolwork, chores, and so on" guideline. You can add "No helping" to this rule, too, when the parents are involved with doing other things that interfere with independence, like selecting the child's clothes, escorting them to the restroom past age three, or helping them with schoolwork. Parents who over-accommodate are notorious for giving lots of helpful reminders, instructions and nudges when their child is best left to figure it out on their own. They also tend to do things for their child and with their child that should not require their assistance, such as accompanying their child as they go to a nearby park to meet a friend. I suggest the parents get a supply of money to have on hand to pay up on the spot when they make mistakes. The child is the judge of whether the parent/caregiver needs to pay. The parent's job is to convince the child they trust their ability to become more independent and skilled on their own and to avoid making their child rich in paid fines.

During subsequent sessions, I acknowledge all steps made by the parent toward promoting independence and asking the child to also give feedback to the parent about their behavior. I want to make the family system self-reinforcing whenever possible. When the parent makes a mistake, I also give feedback. I use the phrases below to make it easier for the parent to feel helped rather than criticized. It helps to remember that parents who over-accommodate are also anxious and worried and likely have a too narrow definition of what good parenting and growing up looks like. They get stuck in their belief that their child needs to feel loved instead of effective. They get focused on helping their child experience visible success instead of learning resilience by discovering how to recover from mistakes. They forget that when they intervene too much, they deny their child the gift of struggle that leads to grit. They may even take pride in their own history of independent struggle yet fear they will put their child at a disadvantage in the competition with other children and feel the need to sculpt their child's successes. Your job is to redirect this misguided attempt to love into a campaign to use the struggle against OCD as their child's opportunity to build inner strength that leads to effective adulthood.

Helpful phrases for offering corrective feedback to parents

"Looks as if you are accidentally making it more difficult for your child when you get tears in your eyes. Are you accidentally feeling sorry for your child? Do you have any idea what I am feeling and how come I am smiling? It's because I am so pleased (name of patient) is doing something difficult and courageous and this means they are on the path to success."

"I can tell you love your child very much and want so much for them to succeed. It looks as if you are accidentally letting your enthusiasm for their success make you think that if they do not get it perfectly right then they will never succeed. What can you say to yourself about how all humans must practice a lot to get more skilled?"

"You just accidentally tried to reassure your child. (Name of patient), can you remind your parent that this is accidentally taking the side of OCD and showing them they cannot handle their OCD by themselves?"

"When you hesitate to do the same exposure (name of patient) is doing, what message are you accidentally sending them? What could you do to face your fear/disgust that shows them a great example of doing challenging things?"

"When you hold your breath, you are accidentally sending the signal that what we are doing is too much for your child and you don't believe (name of patient) can do it. Can you help (name of patient) face their OCD by practicing calming yourself while they are doing something difficult? (Name of patient), can you

---

remind your parent what it feels like to see them get so anxious about you getting anxious?"

Assess sleep habits

OCD worsens when there is sleep deprivation (Harrington *et al.*, 2021). Patients and parents who are sleep deprived either because of OCD, or due to poor sleep habits, have the disadvantage of being less able to handle the rigors of deliberate exposure to OCD triggers. Additionally, many psychiatrists will tell you that chronic sleep deprivation will reduce or nullify the effects of medication (Brand and Kirov, 2011). Therefore, I always ask patients and parents about their sleep habits. If I discover the patient, parents or both are sleep deprived, which is often the case, I prioritize establishing healthy sleep routines when OCD is not the cause of inadequate sleep. When OCD is the cause of inadequate sleep, I prioritize any obsessions and compulsions that interfere with sleep over all others so everyone can more quickly acquire the necessary mental and physical energy to participate in treatment. This includes putting easier-to-treat or other more interfering compulsions to the side in the service of improving sleep. Prioritizing sleep makes everything else easier to manage.

Assess previous treatments

If your patient's OCD is challenging, there is a good chance they have made previous attempts at treatment. What others have attempted and how others have explained the patient's OCD to the patient can become significant when it is inaccurate or incomplete. Here are the questions I ask to help formulate what needs to change to improve the patient's chance of a full recovery:

1. Have you ever tried exposure with response prevention treatment before? What kinds of things did you practice? Were you able to achieve response prevention and not give in to your OCD during your most difficult practices? Did you have home practice? Were you able to do it? Do you think doing ERP helped?

2. How long did you do your ERP? How many sessions a week?

How long did sessions last? Did you experience improvement between sessions? Or only within sessions?

3. What did your therapist do when you were unable to complete an exposure practice?

4. If you take medication, do you think it makes it easier to deal with your OCD? Do you think your child's medication has lessened their symptoms?

5. How willing were you to do treatment? Did oppositional behaviors make it difficult or impossible to complete treatment?

6. What things did you do in your therapy if you were not doing ERP? What did you talk about? What activities did you do?

7. What do you think has made OCD so difficult for you?

8. What is the hardest part about having OCD?

9. What do you think causes your OCD?

10. What do you believe would make things better for yourself? Your child?

11. What seemed to be the most helpful thing you did in previous treatment, even if it did not stick? What was the least helpful?

12. Did you ever do exposures that you felt were too difficult? Did you ever succeed at doing exposure practices that you did not believe you could do?

13. How did you do exposure practice with your therapist? Did they do it with you? Did they just give you instructions for how to do it at home? Did they ever have you do it by yourself?

14. Is there anyone who thinks that you should not do ERP? Is there anyone who thinks that some of the things your therapist said you should do were inappropriate, dangerous, disgusting, blasphemous or wrong for kids to do?

15. For parents only: What do you think makes it easiest for you to give in to your child's OCD? What makes it easiest for your child to give in to their OCD?

16. For parents only: Do you ever do rituals for your child? Or avoid things because of your child's OCD? Or make others in the home do things to avoid triggering your child's OCD? Have you given up important activities because of your child's OCD?

17. For parents only: Do you do anything special to make it easier for your child to live with their OCD, such as sleeping with them or checking a situation ahead of time to see if you can avoid triggers for OCD?

Making sense of the symptoms

Let's assume you have completed your assessment and have as much information as possible. What do you do next to set the stage for success? How do you connect all the patterns of symptoms and outside influences that contribute to your patient's OCD? I begin by prioritizing symptoms based on the level of interference, as opposed to the level of distress. So, instead of trying to rank order all the symptoms in terms of the estimated ease of practice, I try to discern which symptoms are most disruptive, because I have discovered that the symptom relief obtained by doing low-level exposure practices may either be negligible in terms of enhancing motivation or irrelevant in terms of overall distress. Patients with difficult-to-treat subtypes need some early successes to help motivate them to continue and complete treatment. Part of my strategy is to target those symptoms that will give the patient the most leverage against their OCD. This is in keeping with an inhibitory learning strategy that seeks to teach patients that they can handle any symptom at any time without first having to become mentally or emotionally prepared. Additionally, early targeting of symptoms that severely disrupts daily life provides stamina and courage to complete the entirety of treatment. It respects the unique needs of the patient and their family. If a patient is malnourished, sleep deprived or in physical discomfort due to compulsions, they need quick relief to focus on more tedious symptoms. For example, a patient with scrupulosity OCD that involved every aspect of her daily choices and religious practices came into treatment during Lent, the season that precedes Easter. She and her family very much wanted her to be able to receive Holy Communion during Easter even though doing this would entail working on her scariest intrusive thoughts. Both she and her family wanted to start with her scariest thoughts, which required maximal effort on her part.

Similarly, Zane, a teen, had sexual assault obsessions triggered by noticing the sexual body parts of male peers. He had been home-schooled and was about to attend public high school a month after entering my clinic. We knew his gym class would provide rich opportunities for exposure practice and we began treatment with exposure practice in public locker rooms, pools and saunas where he would encounter naked bodies, instead of beginning with easier imaginal exposure and being near peers while looking at their belt buckle or zipper fly.

The list of things I prioritize in treatment are obsessions and compulsions that interfere with:

- life-threatening rituals that prevent eating, drinking, taking life-saving medications or getting life-saving treatments

- the patient or family's sleep

- safety, such as standing for long hours in an attitude of prayer, getting sores on knees from kneeling in prayer, staring at the sun, holding breath, refusing to eat in order to not contribute to global warming, reporting self as a suspected criminal

- important daily activities, such as attending school, fully participating in school

- personal hygiene

- friendships, relationships with family

- finances, such as giving away all money earned to those who are less fortunate, refusing to allow others to spend money on the patient

- everything else, such as schoolwork, chores, sports, leisure time.

After setting up a priority list, I ask the patient to estimate how difficult they think various examples of exposure practice might be for each of the obsessions and compulsions they have reported. You do not need an exact measurement of estimated difficulty, especially since this can often change during treatment, but rather a way to know which exposure practices are likely to require more time, more support or more sessions during the initial phase of treatment. Here are suggestions for obtaining estimated ratings of anxiety from your patients:

Age of patient	Method of assessment
1–4	Smiley face or frowny face emojis
	Thumbs up or thumbs down
	Loudness of tantrum, crying or degree of attempted avoidance
5–7	Set of smiley face emojis that go from crying then sad, then neutral, then small smile, then big smile
	0–10 scale, with 0=best day ever and 10=worst OCD day ever
	Easy peasy, not so bad, bit harder, really hard, impossible
8–10	0–10 scale or 0–100 scale
11 and older	0–100 scale or percentages from 0–100%

Next, you need to be able to describe each obsession and what the patient does to neutralize the obsession with rituals/compulsions, avoidance, reassurance seeking or oppositional behaviors that pose as avoidance. Then you should understand how each compulsion, avoidance or reassurance-seeking ritual functions to reduce anxiety. You should also inquire about whether the patient is doing what I call a responsibility dump. Responsibility dumps are when a patient decreases anxiety by informing someone about their obsession or desire to perform a compulsion, and then assumes that by telling someone else they have transferred the moral obligation of OCD to the listener. Here are some examples of responsibility dumping.

CASE EXAMPLE

Remy got intrusive thoughts about terrible automobile, plane and construction accidents. When he got these obsessions, he wanted to tell others about them so that he was no longer the only one to know these things might happen. When he did this, it felt as though others were looking out for the victims of these accidents in case they happened. He wrote stories about his obsessions and posted online in chat groups where you could share stories and play video games. He felt relief when he saw that others had read his stories because he imagined they would notify the authorities if the events came true. He did this ritual to let the police station or news station know about the potential impending disasters that his OCD imagined.

Parvati liked to get the opinions of others about every decision she made. Her OCD questioned all her decisions to see if they felt right even though she could never clearly specify what constituted feeling right. So long as she was able to ask someone else's opinion, she could follow their opinion and attribute any bad consequences of her decision to the other person, even though she knew this did not make sense. She also discovered that flipping a coin to help make decisions worked as a compulsion because the penny then was the "one" who was right or wrong.

Once I have a clear picture of what the patient does to neutralize their obsessions, then I want to also identify how compulsions, avoidance or seeking reassurance work to reduce anxiety. Do parents, peers, siblings, friends, pets or others play a role in neutralizing OCD? What happens if they do not do their part? I like to ask the patient about each attempt to neutralize OCD, "What would happen if you did not do this? Or if someone else did not do this? What happens if the bad thing happens? What would your OCD say and do?" Their answers can be very informative for identifying information overlooked from the Y-BOCS or clinical interview. In short, I want to learn to think like the patient's OCD thinks so I can design effective ways to dismantle the patient's OCD.

Once I have a clear picture of what worked and failed in previous treatments, what the patient understood or failed to understand about their OCD and I can describe which triggers give rise to compulsions, reassurance seeking, avoidance or avoidance expressed through oppositional behaviors, I am ready to start treatment. Since most patients are still developing their ability to motivate and self-regulate, I always like to have an agreed on reward system with the patient and parents. I will not cover how to set up a reward system in this book, but in the Resources section at the end of this book you can find the reference for my other book that describes this in detail (Cassiday, 2022). Having a good reward system is cheaper, easier and more fun than accidentally prolonging therapy.

The next chapter will help you assess and manage the problem of avoidance that comes in the form of oppositional behaviors. Sometimes the thing that makes a patient's OCD difficult to treat is the patient's poor ability to manage strong emotions, frustration and their parents who have yet to develop effective skills for managing oppositional behaviors and promoting resilience. When you have effective tools to handle oppositionality it will make it easier to treat patients who believe they are unable to face their OCD triggers without compulsions, avoidance and reassurance seeking.

If you would like to view a demonstration of how to implement some of the strategies mentioned in this chapter, please go to https://library.jkp.com/redeem using the code ZVEAZDD.

CHAPTER 3

Effective Ways to Handle Oppositional Behaviors

Oppositional behaviors are common in children with severe and difficult-to-treat subtypes of OCD. Even though the public image of an anxious patient is that of an internalizing disorder typified by timidity, fear of offending, fear of making mistakes and being frozen in fear, some patients end up expressing their anxiety through externalizing behaviors. They get stuck in the fight mode of the fight, flight or freeze response. This can occur in patients who were previously cooperative, polite and willing to do tedious things such as chores. Loud crying and refusing to go to bed, join family activities or attend school are common. Tantrums occur when there is threat of exposure to OCD triggers. Tantrums may involve threatening suicide, self-harm, vandalism or running away, because many patients learn that these threats secure a guaranteed escape from facing triggers while adults complete safety assessments, go to the Emergency Department or seek advice. Some patients become mute or frozen in place to avoid making their obsessions or compulsions worse and their opposition takes the form of the silent, passive protest. The dilemma for many therapists and parents is how to manage these oppositional behaviors, especially when they seem so dramatic and disturbing or indicative of more severe problems.

PANS/PANDAS

The presence of repetitive oppositional behavior suggests several important areas for your consideration before attempting to directly address OCD symptoms. First, an acute onset of oppositional behaviors, especially when accompanied by decreased or loss of appetite or refusal to eat, is indicative of pediatric autoimmune neuropsychiatric syndromes (PANS) or pediatric autoimmune neuropsychiatric disorders associated with streptococcus (PANDAS). Patients who suffer from PANS/PANDAS experience inflammation and infection from viruses or other infections that cross the blood brain barrier. Current science suggests that patients who develop PANS/PANDAS may have inherited defects in their immune system that make them vulnerable to developing OCD following infection from viruses, parasites or bacteria. They may also have less diverse gut bacteria that promote effective immune function (Frankovich, 2022). The initial onset is rapid, usually overnight or within four to five days, with acute onset of severe irritability, tantrums, obsessions and compulsions resulting (Brown *et al.*, 2017). The patient will also have subtle or not so subtle neurological symptoms, such as poor balance, impaired concentration, weakened grip strength and other symptoms that are best assessed by a specialist familiar with PANS/PANDAS. Treatment for OCD caused by PANS/PANDAS should involve medical interventions that focus on decreasing inflammation, eliminating infection, decreasing antibodies to infection and improving immunological function. Patients who have untreated PANS/PANDAS will be poor responders to psychiatric medication and cognitive behavioral interventions until their medical status is stabilized. This means that you should carefully interview any patient you suspect has PANS/PANDAS for history of symptom onset and history of possible symptoms of infection. Patients who do not have these syndromes will have a more gradual onset that does not involve acute presentation of symptoms, irritability, and neurological signs.

You should suspect PANS/PANDAS any time you and your patient's family are doing a good job of intervening and the patient worsens instead of gets better. Some patients who have these syndromes will recover completely or greatly when they are treated during the acute phase of the illness. Those who do not recover completely with medical treatment will need and respond to cognitive behavioral treatment, such as ERP, once they have completed medical intervention. Additionally, some patients will have a flare up in OCD symptoms each time they get an infection or viral illness and will need ongoing medical and behavioral support (O'Dor *et al.*, 2022). Covid-19 infections have also been shown to cause PANS/PANDAS in vulnerable patients (O'Dor *et al.*, 2022). My experience has been that no amount of family intervention for PANS/PANDAS-related oppositional behavior is successful unless you address the medical issue of inflammation and autoimmune response. Research shows that the earlier you intervene, the better the outcome and the ideal window is within one year of the onset of symptoms. The Resources section at the back of this book contains a link for identifying physicians and nurse practitioners who are skilled in assessing and treating PANS/PANDAS-related symptoms and for learning more information about PANS/PANDAS. Here is a list of criteria for diagnosing PANS/PANDAS:

Diagnostic criteria for PANS/PANDAS

1. An abrupt, acute, dramatic onset of obsessive compulsive disorder or severely restricted food intake

---

2. At least two of the following that occur at the same time as the onset of the OCD symptoms and restricted food intake:
   - Anxiety
   - Emotional lability and/or depression
   - Irritability, aggression and/or severe oppositional behaviors
   - Behavioral (developmental) regression, such as bedwetting, being unable to sleep alone or acting much younger
   - Sudden deterioration in schoolwork
   - Motor or sensory abnormalities, such as poor balance, clumsy, disturbed by sounds, tastes or textures
   - Somatic signs and symptoms, including sleep disturbances, bedwetting or frequent urination

---

3. Symptoms that cannot be better explained by another neurologic or medical disorder

---

Practical versus perfect

Even though your patient is seeking treatment for OCD, you may need to initially divert direct treatment of OCD when oppositional behaviors derail attempts at implementing the treatment. For example, if the patient cannot get to your office or leave their home, you will need to pivot and be ready to either help the parents learn how to get the child to treatment or begin treatment in the patient's home. If the patient becomes destructive or aggressive in their attempts to avoid treatment, then you will need to secure everyone's safety before you can increase the patient's anxiety by doing therapeutic exposure tasks. If the patient insists on interrupting treatment with rude comments, then you will have to find a way to keep treatment on track so that swearing, mean comments and implied insults have no traction or ability to derail treatment. Many therapists get stuck at this point because they assume that the problem has to do with a patient who is poorly motivated and/or parents who are unwilling to take charge of their child's unruly behavior. It is helpful to remember that everyone is doing the best they can with what they have. It is your job to re-orient the family system toward teaching resilience instead of accidentally reinforcing avoidance by showing everyone that the fight response of anxiety is just another expression of anxiety that can be overcome. You need to put on the mindset of a veterinarian who knows that some pets will bite and snap in fear regardless of the vet's good intentions and skill at decreasing pain and suffering. This means that you will need to become flexible in the way you work with anxious oppositional patients and let go of the idea of being able to quickly establish rapport, get accurate self-disclosure or even any self-disclosure, and be prepared to put on your mental shield of never personally taking anything a scared, angry patient says when they are intent on escape.

The fight response of anxiety is just another expression of anxiety that can be overcome.

When a patient is determined to hijack assessment and treatment with rude words and refusal to cooperate, it is better to work just with the parents to create a funnel that pushes the patient toward treatment. Direct confrontation from you, or the parents, will only provoke more aggression and is never wise. Many therapists and parents make the mistake of believing they must confront the patient with their foolishness and apparent self-sabotaging behaviors. When someone is scared and does not believe they can cope with anxiety, they are desperately focused on avoidance at all costs. They cannot think clearly about the future, even the near future. They know they are doing inappropriate things and likely feel great shame, which they hide with angry bluster. When parents or therapists accidentally use shame-inducing language, they create more shame, which in turn promotes more avoidance. Showing an example of calm acceptance is very important for both parent and child. How you react to the patient's tantrums and threats will establish the emotional climate for treatment.

Part of being practical is figuring out in which location treatment should begin. If a parent cannot get their child to treatment because they are too large, too clever at running away or quick to threaten suicide or vandalism when the topic of treatment is mentioned, then meeting the child in their home is a better choice. Sometimes the patient will be so destructive with tantrums or protests, the best way to proceed is to coach the parents how to address oppositional behaviors and enforce ERP without the child present during treatment sessions. When the patient is large enough and combative enough that it is unsafe to force them to come to my office, I will go to their home. My goal is to figure out the best place to start instead of getting stuck in my office. Going to the patient's home can be invaluable for learning more about symptoms and problem areas to address, such as how the parents handle their child's oppositional behaviors.

If you have never made a home visit, you might feel concern about your own safety or about how to structure assessment and treatment. My experience with home-delivered therapy is that it can be as effective or more effective than sessions conducted in the office because it allows you to observe the patient in their home setting so you can better identify style of parenting and obstacles to treatment and see typical triggers for the patient's OCD. For example, you might learn the patient's sleeping area is full of digital devices that prevent healthy sleep or see how easy it is for the patient to run away because their sleeping area is closest to the door or has large first-floor windows that cannot be secured. You might discover that there are many fragile, valued objects the parents protect by giving in to tantrums when the patient threatens vandalism. Discovering this information can be invaluable for determining how to intervene and how to prepare to intervene.

If you are concerned about the patient becoming aggressive, there are some helpful suggestions about this that inpatient staff are given when working with unpredictable patients. For example, before going to a patient's home, I first determine if there are any things the parents can do prior to the meeting that would make things safer, such as packing away objects that are potential projectiles or weapons or that are special and therefore potential targets for vandalism. I also ask for siblings to either be away or in an area that is out of sight and hearing of my meeting with the patient. This often means during the school day or when preschool is in session. I want the parents, patient and myself to be free of distraction. I also ask the parents to secure any easy outdoor exits, such as doors or windows, so the patient's best option for escape is to their sleeping area. Lastly, I give them a script for how to explain my visit and suggest that they let their child know several days before about my visit. The script is like this:

Therapist: "Please do not surprise your child by telling them right before my visit that I am coming. This will erode their trust in you at a time in which they need your calm strength to make the journey to recovery. You need to show them you are not afraid of their anxious anger. You are just being practical. Here is how you can tell them about my visit.

I know your anxiety has been making you miserable and difficult to live with. I love you and want you to learn how to become free of OCD. I also know that your OCD has fooled you into believing that you cannot possibly do treatment or that there is no one who can possibly help you get better. I know that is a lie and I know you can get better. That is why (name of therapist) is coming to our house to talk to you and help us all get started on the journey to overcoming OCD. It's okay if you are scared, mad or extremely mad. It's not okay for us to do nothing. If you had cancer and hated needles, we would still make you do treatment. It's the same with OCD. What do you think?

"Then, I instruct the parents to just agree with every distressed statement their child makes.

Yes, it is unfair that we invited the therapist to come see you without your permission.

You're right, we did not first ask you and that makes you extremely angry. I bet you feel betrayed.

Yes, we are really annoying and have no true understanding of your OCD.

Yes, you are right. Your life really does suck.

Yes, I can see why you wish you could die.

"I explain that the goal is to just calmly express empathy, so the child feels deeply understood, though not persuaded. Do not try to persuade the child to cooperate with the visit or to be nice to the therapist. That is more likely to escalate the conflict. Encourage the parents to accept that a home visit is not on their child's list of fun things to do. Parents can also offer a reward for meeting with the therapist, such as guaranteeing screen time, choosing the dinner or dessert for the night or having a special activity. If the child refuses rewards, do not try to find one; just continue to empathize and avoid negotiating about the visit. If this is done correctly, it will take the edge off the patient's anger and decrease the likelihood of them having a tantrum, running away or sitting silently."

Here is advice for therapists unfamiliar with making home visits to potentially anxious and angry patients:

- Allow the patient an easy exit so they can avoid feeling threatened or trapped.

- Wear comfortable clothing and footwear so you can move readily.

- Choose to exit rather than confront the patient if your presence is provoking physical aggression.

- Have a neutral zone where you can talk with the parents or family apart from the patient.

- Be sure to empathize with the patient and tell them, "I know this must feel really awkward or even embarrassing to have me in your home. I can see why you feel so angry and upset. It looks as if your OCD is really messing up your life if things got to this point. I would be upset too, if I were in your shoes."

- Be willing to talk to them through the door instead of face to face.

Once in the home, I introduce myself to the patient at whichever location they are, even if it is behind a closed bedroom or bathroom door. I let them know that I am glad to meet them and that if they are like my previous patients who were reluctant to go to therapy, I can see how annoying it must be to have me come to their home. I also invite them to tell me what makes it so difficult to have to meet with me so I can immediately work on building rapport by allowing the patient to complain about the adults instead of what they expected, which was to have the adults complain about them. Once they are done complaining and show they feel understood by backing off their anger, I introduce myself and explain what I hope to accomplish. If they are willing to complain about me or the parents, then I consider this a good sign, since they are engaging with me as opposed to sitting silently or hiding and being silent.

If the patient refuses to talk, or to be in my presence, I simply do the same thing, but move into the introduction and explanation for my visit. My introduction might go like this:

Therapist: "I am really glad you have been willing to be honest with me about how frustrating it is to have to meet with me. That shows a lot of courage and ability to know what you want.

Most kids I get to work with usually hate having to meet with me at first and sometimes even hate me. That is no surprise because they had really difficult OCD that convinced them the only way to feel better was to either do what the OCD told them, to get others to do what the OCD wanted or to avoid anything that might trigger their OCD. They were so bossed by OCD they were miserable and really irritable. They even had horrible fits of screaming, pushing, hitting, breaking things or saying they wanted to die. It sounds like that might have been happening to you. Does this sound like anything you recognize?"

Patient: "Maybe."

Therapist: "Do you want to know what those other kids felt like after I worked with them and taught them how to fight back against their OCD?"

Patient is silent, but looks curious.

Therapist: "They were proud of what they could do, and they even told me they were glad they did therapy! It sounds kind of shocking, doesn't it? They went to this from hating me and hating therapy, kind of like how soldiers feel about their commander after they go through boot camp. Do you know what boot camp is? Have you ever heard about it?"

Patient: "Sort of."

Therapist: "Boot camp is where you do the hardest training and most difficult things, so you are prepared for battle. The army does boot camp so soldiers can be prepared to do anything when they are really scared in battle. It's kind of like what we will do when we work together to help you win the battle over your OCD. What do you think about that idea? If you want, I can tell you about some other kids like you and what they did to overcome their OCD. Would you like that?"

My motivation for talking about other kids who were oppositional and overcame OCD is to provide inspiration and a positive role model for the patient. Often, when patients are oppositional, they are terrified because they cannot imagine how they might endure or overcome their OCD. Hearing stories of hope can do much to instill the beginning of realistic hope, which builds willingness to try. I also offer to show the child real stories of similar children, teens or young adults with similar symptoms by looking up stories from the International OCD Foundation or on YouTube. Once the patient has expressed interest in hearing about others like them, I can proceed to asking them questions about their symptoms.

When I have children or teens who detest coming into treatment but are compliant with coming to my location, I offer the bargain of meeting less after they prove they can do exposure with response prevention and prove they can do their home practice without prompting. I let them know that if they can convince me and their caregivers that they have met each session's goals, then they can earn their way out of having to meet with me in person or in my office.

When the patient refuses to participate in treatment by being silent or sitting behind a closed door, I make sure I let them know that treatment will proceed, but it may become prolonged or extra annoying because I will not have the best information as only the patient knows all the details of their OCD. I mention that I might end up making them do things that are unnecessary, boring or extra irritating because I do not have the full picture, but it is their choice to decide how efficient or difficult they want their treatment to become. Then I exit and continue the meeting with the parents. If the patient is willing to begin by talking to me behind a closed door, I begin my introduction and assessment and only ask for the door to be opened once they appear to be answering in more detail. If the patient joins the session by coming out of the room or volunteering to talk, I act as though nothing happened and start asking them questions or getting clarification of information. I want to make their entry into treatment a face-saving one that does not put undue attention on their oppositional behavior. I also let them know how helpful their self-disclosure is by saying things such as, "That is a great insight," or, "You described that well. It's easy for me to see how your OCD got you to this difficult point," or, "No wonder you did not want to meet with me. Your OCD has been making your life miserable." I coach the parents to avoid making comment when the child joins us and to just relax until the end of the session when they should then tell their child, "I am proud you took a courageous step by helping us figure out how to better help you. Way to go."

The formula I use for talking with patients who are refusing to cooperate is the following:

1. Say aloud what they likely feel and why.

2. Let them know they are not alone.

3. Let them know that assessment and treatment will proceed regardless of their participation.

4. Let them know their participation will speed up treatment and make treatment less annoying.

5. Give a forced choice to either talk with you from the location where they are stuck or to join you with their parents.

Here are some examples of how this might sound:

Child's behavior	Your calm empathic response
Patient refuses to get out the car to come into the office	You go to the car and say, "Looks as if you are really scared and mad because you cannot imagine how to do treatment or how treatment could help. Lots of kids with OCD have got stuck in the parking lot and then discovered that they could overcome their OCD and get their lives back step by step. I would love to tell you more about that. I can understand why you hate your parents and me right now, but that is just your OCD hijacking you into believing that we are the enemy instead of your OCD. You can join us in my office if you want, or I can meet with you here in the parking lot. Which would you prefer?"
The patient screams at you, "You and my parents are ****ing idiots! I am not doing this!"	You give a calm friendly smile and say, "Looks as if you are furious with us. It seems as if your OCD has been controlling you and harassing you terribly. I know your parents and I cannot possibly understand exactly how difficult it feels to be in your shoes right now. What we do understand is that you are not free to be yourself because of your OCD. Lots of kids who come to my clinic have hated their parents and therapists because their OCD took control. They discovered they could get back in charge, one step at a time. I would love to tell you about those kids or even let you talk to one of them who felt just like you so you can find out for yourself. What I cannot do is just let OCD ruin your life. It would be no different from standing by while cancer killed you because you would not get treatment due to a fear of needles and medicine. What do you think?"

cont.

Child's behavior	Your calm empathic response
The patient will not come out of their room to talk to you face to face	You talk loudly through the door and say, "I wouldn't want to meet a total stranger who says she is a therapist either. Unfortunately, I cannot change that you appear to have a horrible case of OCD and that I am a therapist who treats OCD. If you can come out and talk with me, I could better understand what is going on and do a better job designing treatment that goes faster and better for you. If you stay in there and don't talk to me, then I run the risk of making mistakes that will make your life even more annoying than it already is. I am leaving now to talk with your parents"
The patient tries to run out of your office	You do the following: stand between the patient and the door, forming a body block and say, "If you leave, I run the risk of screwing up your treatment because I only have what your parents tell me. I know that you know that parents are usually not well informed about what is going on in their child's mind. I can tell that you are mad and scared and that is typical for how OCD can wreck your life. Would you like to hear about other kids just like you who have hated their therapist, treatment and parents and still been able to get better?"

OCD ambassadors

One way to help anxious, angry, avoidant patients agree to treatment is to help them hear real-life stories of initial treatment refusal and eventual success. I regularly ask my patients who have made progress in treatment if they would be interested in volunteering to encourage other patients who are afraid to begin treatment. Most kids love the idea of helping others, especially when it involves being the one who is the inspiration for others. I get the agreement of the parents and then arrange for the patient who has overcome their anxious anger to text or email the avoidant patient and begin a dialogue. I let the patients choose how much they want to communicate or even if they want to meet each other. I offer my office as a place to meet. I also encourage reluctant patients to read stories of struggle and success from OCD-related websites or YouTube videos. This has always proved to be helpful in wearing down the patient's disbelief in their ability to handle treatment and OCD. If there are nearby support groups that include patients similar in age and severity to my patient's OCD, then

I recommend attendance at one of these virtual or in-person groups. Remember, the easiest way to get inspired is to hear the story of someone who is similar and a few steps ahead of you in skill. Developing a group of OCD ambassadors for treatment is much more relatable for a young patient than an adult saying, "Trust me. I really am an expert." Social learning theory shows us that another child, teen or young adult will have a greater capacity to influence a reluctant patient than a very skilled therapist (Morgenroth *et al.*, 2015). Additionally, there is no lonelier feeling than that of believing you are unique in your suffering. Even young children benefit from knowing they are not alone. A parent's love or therapist's skill and good intentions cannot compensate for knowing someone shares your struggle.

When plan A and plan B fail

What happens when you have tried everything previously mentioned and the patient continues to refuse treatment or works hard to disrupt treatment sessions? The choice is simple. Start treatment without them and work with their parents, school and other healthcare providers to funnel them into ERP. This may sound absurd, since most therapists presume treatment can only proceed when the patient is cooperative, verbal and willing to talk. If you accidentally have bought into this assumption, I would like to challenge your thinking. If you have worked with developmentally delayed or disabled children, then you already know how to intervene when your patients lack the capacity to understand, consent or participate in treatment in a helpful manner. The dilemma is that in the case of severe OCD, it is OCD that interferes with the patient's ability to participate in treatment, along with their developmental maturity. Like working with developmentally challenged patients, you will have to rely on your understanding of OCD, its subtypes and your powers of observation and inference. Your patient's behavior will show you what situations, words and behaviors they fear. What they avoid will become your compass. What they do to avoid and neutralize accidental exposure to feared sensations, situations or people will give you the necessary clues to design and implement treatment. I continually offer the patient the opportunity to participate as treatment progresses and typically, they do.

When patients are expert refusers, I look for ways to impose exposure practice and response prevention that do not require their cooperation. I also coach the parents on how to do active ignoring of the patient's oppositional behaviors and how to reframe their child's opposition. For example, if a patient has made the family avoid saying certain words or doing certain activities, then I will coach the parents to notify their child that they will be fading out their accommodation and fading in exposure to the words, phrases and activities that trigger OCD, and they will no longer give reassurance. Then the parents begin doing things the patient has previously coerced them into avoiding. In this situation, the parents are assigned the hierarchy of ERP tasks based on everyone's best observations and inferences of the symptoms. Here is a case example of how treatment might look when the patient refuses to cooperate.

CASE EXAMPLE

Petra, a 13-year-old trans girl who was taking puberty-suppressing hormones, began convincing her parents to avoid using any words that referred to boys, male genitalia or stereotypically male activities or articles (such as boxer shorts, penis, dude, guys, masculine, male, beard, mustache), shortly after she began taking hormones. Petra had been asking her parents for about a year if she really was a girl, to which they had to reply, "Yes" or else she would cry, sob and beg them to say the right answer with the correct enthusiastic inflection until she felt satisfied with their answer. This request for the right answer could last for 30–60 minutes until it felt just right. Her intrusive thoughts consisted of ideas such as, "If I agree with those words/activities, then I will switch back to a boy. If they say that, it means that I am not a real girl. If I think about when I dressed like a boy, I will forever give up being a girl." She had loud screaming tantrums whenever her parents slipped and said the wrong words or did things that pertained to maleness, such as her dad shaving his face in sight of his daughter. She also had stopped affectionate contact with her father because he reminded her of masculine things. She ran away and hid after accusing her parents of being mean and wanting her to die because they would not embrace her female nature. She had grabbed knives and scratched her wrists horizontally on several occasions and had been taken to the Emergency Department but never admitted to the inpatient unit. She had also torn her room apart in an anxious rage and refused to go to school, telling her parents, "You ruined my life. You know I cannot focus if I am worrying about being a boy. I can't do school because of you." She would scream when she believed one of her parents was about to say something she feared. She refused treatment, even though she realized her thoughts were a product of her OCD. She so feared the idea of reverting back to the status of living as a boy that she worried, "What if it becomes true that I really am a boy?"

Petra's parents had been coached by therapists skilled with transitions in LGBTQ+ to accommodate and provide reassurance to the patient because in the LGQ+ community it is commonly understood that living as the wrong gender can be traumatic. It was assumed that her reaction was a traumatic response to seeing maleness in her body. Her well-intentioned therapists also warned the parents about the very real elevated risk for suicide in trans youth. This gave the parents further impetus to accommodate avoidance of all things male. She refused treatment on the grounds that I misunderstood LGBTQ+ patients. She said she just wanted more time on her own to get past her trauma before she addressed her OCD. She knew her LGBTQ+ therapist was skeptical about my proposed treatment because I lacked expertise in LGBTQ+ issues. The parents saw her symptoms worsening and feared her doing something that would lead to suicide.

Her parents were so exhausted and demoralized they felt unable to battle with their child to bring her into my office, so I went to their home. Prior to their visit, I asked them to hide all knives and sharp objects. I coached the parents to ignore her and to focus on working with me on how to handle her tantrums with active ignoring. I also reminded them that although their daughter's behaviors were extreme, she had not actually had a serious suicide attempt but was rather expressing her fear with the fight component of the fight, flight or freeze response. When I arrived, the patient hid in her room, earbuds plugged into her ears, playing loud music, and refused to acknowledge my presence. I introduced myself and told her I would like to have her help understanding her OCD and designing treatment and then I left her room. Shortly after her parents and I began meeting, Petra ran into the room yelling and screaming that we should leave her alone and let her die. I responded by saying, "I can tell that you are really scared and really stuck. It must feel awful to see us figuring out how to fight your OCD and not know what we are planning. Perhaps you could join us to help us get it right?" She then began to scream more, refusing to leave the room and declaring, "No one is going to make me do anything! **** all of you!" My response was to ignore her and to ask her parents to go with me to their car. We sat inside their car while locking her out, ignoring her and discussing how to proceed. We then drove away when she began hitting the car as I coached the parents to avoid eye contact or any visible reaction to their daughter.

We decided together that we would start treatment by refusing to offer reassurance and agreed to next meet in my office without their daughter so we could plan and practice in peace. Thirty-five minutes later, we returned home to find that the daughter had stopped scream-ing but stood glaring at us through the windshield, which we ignored. While in the car, I role-played arguing with the parents in the manner the patient did while they practiced saying, "Looks as if your OCD is making you scared and angry," then ignoring her and turning away. I instructed the parents to use this response until we next met in person.

I met with the parents weekly over the next several months, sending a text to the patient inviting her to join us and help make treatment more to her liking. Each session, the parents chose an accommodating behavior to eliminate, and we role-played handling the likely tantrum that would ensue. We began posting feared words and concepts around the house on post-it notes and posters, first in the common family areas and then in her room, bathroom and on her belongings and the snacks she preferred. Her tantrums gradually decreased during this two-month period. She would grumble and glare when she noticed new words. She gave up trying to remove the signs and post-its once she realized her parents would repost everything she pulled down and otherwise ignore her. When we notified her that the next step in treatment was for her par-ents to begin using the words she feared in conversation, and they would soon place boys' underwear on all her belongings, she chose to meet with us at the office. She admitted the parent-based exposure was effective and was willing to try treatment on her own. Subsequently she was able to look at anxiety-provoking pictures of male clothing, males in bathing suits and boys playing "male" sports. She was able to repeat feared words and to make exposure statements such as, "I hope and pray with all my heart I am not really a girl." Ultimately, she succeeded in losing her fear of her intrusive thoughts, stopped all tantrums and no longer gave in to compulsions to avoid things related to males.

It is important to teach parents to ignore oppositional behaviors and express empathy without accidentally resorting to accommodating behaviors for the sake of calming the patient or avoiding conflict. Be sure to use ample role play with parents to verify they can handle any difficult situation their child might deliver.

Physical prompts

Sometimes, it may be necessary to use physical prompts to keep a child from hitting, biting or attacking a therapist, pet or parent when they have severe tantrums. If safe restraint is not part of your past experience, I recommend you get training so you can teach the parents how to safely restrain their child to prevent the patient from hurting themselves, others or the environment. The dilemma with aggressive behaviors is that the more someone uses them, the more disinhibited they become about using the next more extreme behavior. It is also humiliating to become the person whom others fear because of loss of temper. I consider it necessary for the mental health and safety of patients to make efforts to prevent further harmful oppositional behaviors. Patients always tell me after they make progress in treatment that they hated being out of control and doing such egregious things. They just didn't know how to avoid acting that way.

When refusal behaviors threaten the patient's life

Sometimes OCD can result in extreme avoidance that threatens the patient's life or prevents self-care. When patients are unable to eat, drink, dress or move, you may need to use prolonged ERP sessions (twice daily three to four hours at a time), hand-over-hand prompting and, when necessary, medical intervention to prevent dangerous dehydration or starvation. When patients cannot dress or move so they can't do necessary tasks such as using the toilet, eating or changing positions, I use a hand-over-hand technique such as you use with a small child to help them eat or dress. The parents assist while I help the patient move. I encourage the parents to take over after I demonstrate how to assist the patient to do the thing they fear, such as tasting food, looking at feared situations or moving. You may need to use very graduated exposure for severe refusal to move by encouraging a micro-movement, or gently assisting the patient to make a tiny movement. When patients have become immobilized, I repeatedly remind them of how they deserve to become free to do anything at any time.

> Therapist: "I know this is really difficult and the part of you who is not your OCD wishes you could move and not have to think about all the bad things that will happen if you go against your OCD. You deserve to be free, to make any choice you want and to move any way you want. That is why we are doing this. Let's keep going. I know you can do it and I know we can help you overcome your OCD."

When the patient has lost substantial weight due to refusal to eat or drink, I use a small squirt bottle with a straw to help them first feel a tiny drop of liquid or smoothie on their lips and then their tongue while allowing them to spit out the beverage. The initial goal is to get used to saying "No" to the OCD and to have food or liquid present. I ask the patient to attempt to touch a tiny particle of the food/liquid to their tongue and to spit it out, and then gradually increase the size of the particle until they can taste it. I use repeated and frequent encouragement for each tiny step. I also repeatedly describe how each small step is pushing back their OCD. My criterion for using hand-over-hand assistance, such as someone does when teaching a small child, is when all other methods for cooperation have failed because the patient is so fearful of going against their OCD. I also offer to be the one who gets the blame from the OCD in the early steps so the patient can practice giving in to the movement, eating or drinking while diminishing the moral responsibility of going against the OCD. Experience has shown me that often patients who refuse to move, eat or drink have severe scrupulosity OCD, severe obsessions about making right choices, or severe harming obsessions. For example, a patient fears making a choice to get dressed because their OCD tells them that every choice they make will kill their family, or a patient refuses to eat because their

OCD tells them they have not been properly pious. I will describe more specifically how to handle these situations in later chapters.

Patients like these are impervious to rewards, consequences or offered support because their OCD has convinced them they cannot handle the consequences of failing to get it right according to the rules of their OCD. They have lost their freedom to choose, and believe that nothing is worse than violating the rules of OCD. They will both indicate they want to recover from OCD and completely give in to their OCD. Typically, they will have a history of always giving in to rituals. When talking to parents of these kind of patients, I remind the parents that no child wants to suffer from severe OCD and deeply desires freedom from their symptoms. Treatment is a way to act on behalf of the patient's better self that is imprisoned inside their OCD. I view using hand-over-hand assistance as a form of showing the patient that resistance to OCD is possible, even when they cannot take the first action. It is a way to show the patient they have another choice because once they are made to take the first tiny step, they see that although they are anxious, life continues and nothing terrible occurs. I repeatedly remind them they deserve to overcome OCD and to do what others do so freely. I tell them they can learn to fight back and reclaim their life. I praise them when they decrease physical struggle and point out how they are indeed fighting back by giving in. Here is an example of the conversation with a patient who refused to get dressed because his obsessions would declare every choice he made to be one that guaranteed the death of his grandparents and dog:

Therapist: "I know you must be worried about what your OCD is going to say if we do exposure practice today. Do you remember when we talked about how no matter how hard you try, you cannot wish a million pounds to show up in your piggy bank?"

Patient: "Yes."

Therapist: "Well, just like wishing for something wonderful can't make it happen, having an OCD thought that creates a bad wish cannot make it happen."

Patient: "Yes, but what if it does?"

Therapist: "It sounds as if your OCD is already trying to fool you again. OCD always says, 'but what if...' That is why we are going to do exposure practice by helping you get dressed so you can get used to hearing your OCD's what ifs and not give in to them. The more you practice that the easier it will become to see how OCD is a liar. So, let's go. Let's start with you looking at your sock. I want you to look at it and tell me what your OCD says."

Patient: "Oh no. I can't do that. If I wear that sock my dog might die. That sock is grey and my dog has grey hair. It's about his death."

Therapist: "Fantastic! This is a really good sock for exposure practice then. Could you please touch the sock with your tiniest toe?"

Patient: "No! That would kill my dog. I can't."

Therapist: "It sounds as if your OCD is really trying to scare you. How about I touch the sock and move it closer to your tiniest toe? Let's see if this bothers your OCD?"

Patient: "No (moves foot away). I can't!"

Therapist: "Your OCD sounds as if it is the dictator today and wants to keep you in cold feet. I know you wish you did not have OCD. Which would be easier, you move your toe toward the sock, or I move your toe toward the sock?"

Patient: "I can't kill my dog. You do it!"

Therapist: "Okay, would it be easier if I move the sock toward your toe or your toe toward the sock?"

Patient: "Move the sock."

Therapist: "Okay (moves the sock a bit closer to patient's foot). Is that because I made the move, and you did not have to make the choice?"

Patient: "Yes, my dog still might die, but maybe not as much."

Therapist: "I will move it a bit closer and this time I want you to wave your toe at the sock, just not toward it. Can you do that?"

Patient: "No."

Therapist: "Okay, how about I help your toe move the tiniest bit; that way it's not all the way your fault if something bad happens. Could you do it halfway like that, so you can get used to it?"

Patient: "Yes."

One technique I rely on is to keep things moving once we overcome the initial inertia of beginning ERP. I like to use lots of repeated sets of simple exposure steps, such as opening and closing eyes. I am taking advantage of learning theory that shows lots of repeated practice is better than one big moment of practice. Repeated reinforcement of approximations of the desired behavior, such as briefing holding open a patient's eyes until they participate, leads to success. It's also easier to move forward after you are already in motion. Think of the shove it takes to move a car with a dead battery versus the push it takes once the car is moving. When forcing cooperation, I repeatedly decrease pressure and lessen restraint to allow the patient the opportunity to cooperate in tiny increments while praising them for their effort. I resume safe restraint or pressure to move when the patient resumes the struggle, ebbing and flowing with their level of cooperation. I also remind them why cooperating is important and the best way to gain freedom from OCD.

Here are some examples of types of compulsions that may need physical assistance:

Compulsion	Physical assistance/competing action
Closed eyes/ refusing to look/see	Briefly open eyelids in single-second intervals, then build up to longer intervals
Refusing to eat/drink	Use easy and fun to taste, melt or swallow foods/liquids (mini chocolate candies, ice-cream, smoothies, icing, pudding) that can be placed inside the child's cheek, using tickling to help the child open their mouth while someone quickly uses a squirt bottle to squirt liquids inside their mouth. Do this repeatedly until the child begins to cooperate

cont.

Compulsion	Physical assistance/competing action
Unable to move/walk/ gesture	Have one person help move limbs while the other props the child up—be like the strings on a marionette puppet that help the child move in response to exposure statements, exposure questions or commands
Unable to dress	Use the hand-over-hand technique in which you place the child's hand on their clothing and place your hand on top while assisting them to dress
Unable to do personal hygiene	Use the hand-over-hand technique for washing, bathing, tooth brushing, brushing hair, shaving (use an electric shaver to avoid accidental cuts), toileting
Unable to make choices	Offer a forced exposure choice and use hand-over-hand techniques to indicate the child's opinion by making their hand wave and then making them complete the choice. Tickle the child and use their gestures to indicate a choice and then make the child do that choice, e.g. you moved so that must mean you want... _____
Unable to talk	Pick something that you know the patient would violently disagree with to see if you can provoke them to say, "No!" For example, for scrupulosity OCD focused on perfectly loving God: "Well, I guess if you stay quiet, then it means that you really do not love God and you want to live in Hell for all eternity," or for harming OCD that focuses on never causing harm and being perfectly kind: "Being quiet must mean that you really do not care about (fill in with the patient's compulsion)"

Helping parents stop nagging

Some parents find it very difficult to stop nagging their children to address their OCD. They repeatedly ask them annoying questions that make their child feel patronized or belittled, such as "Have you done your exposure practice yet? How is your OCD now? Are you giving in to your OCD? Shouldn't you do more of your exposure practice?" This is counterproductive because it teaches the child to rely on the parent to discriminate when they need to act against OCD. It undermines skill building in self-awareness and using adaptive coping skills. It also tends to make children assume that their parent's anger or worry is the problem rather than their OCD. For example, if you get stopped for driving too fast and the police are rude, which do you focus on, the fact that you were rushing or the annoying qualities of the constable?

Now that you have an assortment of tools to assess symptoms and to handle the opposition that can occur with severe and difficult-to-treat subtypes of OCD, you are ready to begin addressing the nuances of successful treatment for the challenging subtypes of OCD. Each of the following chapters will describe the challenging aspects of understanding and treating specific difficult-to-treat subtypes so you can approach your work with these challenging patients with calm confidence and practical knowledge.

If you would like to view a demonstration of how to implement some of the strategies mentioned in this chapter, please go to https://library.jkp.com/redeem using the code ZVEAZDD.

CHAPTER 4

Treating Scrupulosity OCD

Religious Obsessions and Compulsions

Scrupulosity OCD that focuses on religious practice and matters of faith can be difficult to treat because many OCD triggers hinge on nuanced issues of the theology and culture of the patient's religious community. Often there will be others of the same denomination who accidentally encourage the patient to be scrupulous because they fail to grasp the nature of the patient's OCD. My working definition for a healthy faith practice is the following: *healthy faith is your ability to effectively tolerate doubt*. My goal in treatment is to use therapy to help patients develop a normal healthy ability to maintain faith despite uncertainty about and an inability to prove the presence of God, spiritual beings or the afterlife or to verify past significant religious events. All faiths call on their participants to make assumptions about things unseen or what happens after death. It is normal for people to build and maintain religious practices. International estimates of belief in God or an afterlife vary from a low of 9% in China to 83% in South Africa (Jones, 2022; Tamir, Connaughton & Salazar, 2020). Approximately 83% of people believe in an afterlife even when they do not believe in God or practice an established religion (Tamir *et al.*, 2020). Treatment for a patient with religious scrupulosity is about both eliminating OCD and helping the patient establish a healthy religious practice that is consonant with their family's or their chosen religion.

Healthy faith is the ability to effectively tolerate doubt.

Some patients will be part of religious communities with a style of faith that appears to have scrupulous underpinnings. Others will be part of religious communities that appear to identify doubt and uncertainty as a normal part of faith. More conservative religions that prescribe strict adherence to rules for daily living, or religions that focus on sincerity of intention, may offer more obvious opportunities for OCD to be triggered due to the doubting nature of OCD. Conservative religious communities, however, are *not* filled with people who have OCD. Conservative religious communities experience the same rates of OCD diagnosis as do non-religious communities (Grisham *et al.*, 2011). Regardless of the religious background of the patient, it is important to understand that *participation in a faith community is not a risk factor for OCD* (Greenberg & Huppert, 2010), and OCD, never the tenets of faith or religion, is always the problem. The dilemma for the patient is that OCD has chosen the field of faith as a battleground. This is important to understand because many mental health professionals who do not observe the same religious practices as their scrupulous OCD patients tend to forget that OCD is hijacking religious observance because they find the patient's faith community's practices inscrutable or nonsensical.

Once you realize that OCD and not the patient's religion is the problem, it makes it easier to identify targets for intervention. Once you also accept that developing a healthy relationship with matters of faith is the goal of treatment, it makes it easier to formulate exposure with response prevention in the same way you would to manage easier-to-treat variants of OCD, such as contamination OCD. Just as you would have zones of no contact for contamination, such as dousing oneself with pesticides, radioactive materials or creating real exposure to HIV, you might have similar areas of non-contact in matters of faith, depending on the patient's faith community. A mainstream protestant church typically would have minimal concern about blasphemous behaviors, such as thinking curse words while in church, because they assume God forgives anything and they do not consider obsessions to ever be blasphemous. An orthodox Jewish community, however, would always find it unacceptable to expose a naked body to a photo of a highly revered rabbi. For the former patient, deliberately thinking curse words during worship would be appropriate, but for the latter patient, keeping the light on in the bathroom and having the door cracked while undressing, while being aware that a portrait of a revered rabbi is exposed to the crack of light from the slightly open bathroom door, would be the appropriate exposure practice. The patient is not exposing their nakedness directly to the revered portrait while allowing reflected light to escape the bathroom. This would be similar to the normal respectful behavior of the faith community toward a special portrait.

Having a framework for intervention also makes it easier to work with scrupulosity OCD. It helps to be able to identify not only the patient's obsessions and compulsions, but also the matters of faith that OCD has distorted or misunderstood. You will need to help the patient contrast what would be the standard perception and practice of an average member of their faith community of their developmental age with what their scrupulosity imposes. When the patient or parents are concerned because you are not a member of their faith community, you need to be willing to find a religious authority to guide your intervention. Additionally, you need to be especially vigilant for intolerance or uncertainty in the patient and reassurance-seeking thoughts and behaviors throughout treatment. Here is an outline of this framework to help guide your intervention.

Questions for building a framework for intervention

1. Are there any obsessions or compulsions that are distortions, exaggerations or outright misapplications of faith that are typical for the patient's faith community? Do you understand this sufficiently to help the patient discriminate between healthy faith and unhealthy or unreasonable acts of OCD? Can you clearly understand and explain to the patient what a healthy acceptance of human imperfection, frailty and inability to control thought and emotion look like in terms that are compatible with their faith community?

2. What would an average person of the patient's age and developmental level be expected to think and do if they had the same religious concern but did not have OCD? How would they react, think and act? What would be considered normal by others in their faith community?

3. How familiar are you with this patient's faith community? Do you understand the nuances of theology or observance enough to direct the patient's exposure practice or do you need an authority to educate and advise you?

4. Does the patient or family accept your intervention, or do you need a religious authority to condone or recommend treatment? Do you need special dispensation to conduct ERP with this patient? For example, do you need a rabbi to lessen rules of observance for the patient because they have OCD? Do you need clarification of how to follow rules of observance?

5. Can you categorize the patient's obsessions and intrusive thoughts as being either intolerance of uncertainty or fear of a bad outcome? Can you categorize the patient's rituals as being acts to obtain certainty, as prevention of a bad outcome or just fear of getting uncontrolled anxiety?

The role of clergy

Having a helpful religious authority endorse treatment and clarify principles of healthy faith and lifestyle can be vital for making headway with patients who have poor insight due to severe anxiety or anxious misinterpretation of holy writings. Almost all religious communities have designated leaders, scholars or theologians who are granted the authority to explain important theological concepts and applications of faith to lifestyle. I work with many patients whose faith community is different from my own. Many patients and their families incorrectly fear recovery will mean having to give up their faith when they hear about the concept of exposure with response prevention. They misunderstand response prevention as having to forego religious practice or assume exposure will involve things unacceptable to their faith community. Having a religious authority who understands OCD or is willing to learn about OCD so they can properly guide treatment makes it much easier to fashion exposure and response prevention that is theologically and therapeutically sound. Most clergy have had some training in mental health and instantly recognize scrupulosity OCD when I describe it, even when they are not familiar with OCD or the word scrupulosity. When I consult with clergy, I make sure to explain my goal of eliminating OCD and restoring or building a healthy faith that leads to the benefit of good mental wellness, good relationships and comfortable belonging in a well-knit faith community. I make sure to mention that I want the patient to learn to live in the messy human middle of accepting uncertainty while assuming God's good grace, the forward progression of their reincarnations, or the peaceful acceptance of things mystical so they can focus on living a joyful life.

Clergy can be very helpful for dealing with the following common topics that trip up most patients with scrupulosity OCD:

1. Defining steps for attaining good standing with God and/or the faith community.

2. Defining the purpose and role of good works.

3. Defining the permanence of one's good status with God.

4. Defining the nature of God (loving versus punitive).

5. Defining degrees of religious observance and ways to do exposure with response prevention while maintaining religious observance.

6. Defining God's forgiveness, mercy and love.

7. Describing how the symptoms of OCD are never a punishment or infliction caused by God.

8. For Christians: How anyone who is concerned with God cannot also commit the unforgivable sin of blaspheming against God. Theologians consider the unpardonable sin mentioned in Matthew 12:31–32 to be that of never acknowledging or recognizing God and living a life that has no concern for God.

9. Emphasizing the good attributes of God or of the faith community that OCD is ignoring or distorting.

For example, a conservative Christian pre-teen girl had obsessions about sinning and failing to be grateful to God if she had a moment of consciousness that did not include simultaneously acknowledging God and being grateful to God. If she noticed a pretty sunset without acknowledging God as the creator and thanking God, then her OCD accused her of sinning. Her OCD began when she heard a youth group lesson from the New Testament scripture, "in all things give thanks" (I Thessalonians 5:16–18, The Holy Bible). Since that time, she had been trying harder each day to constantly feel and think grateful thoughts for everything that crossed her consciousness to the point that she could not focus on anything and constantly froze her movement and speech to focus and not advance to the next thought before being properly grateful. Her peers in the youth group, on the other hand, appeared to be unaffected after the lesson and had repeatedly told her to "stop being so weird." I consulted with the youth group leader to verify his purpose in teaching the lesson, which was to encourage the youth of the church to learn an attitude of gratitude toward God. I asked for his input and he agreed to talk to the patient and explain how she had misunderstood his lesson as a literal instruction in impossible mind control rather than encouragement to learn an attitude which did not require constant action, only a general awareness. He also said he would tell her to do her ERP regardless of what her OCD told her about foregoing response prevention.

Tolerating uncertainty

In the previous example of the pre-teen girl, it was the patient's anxious approach to eliminating uncertainty and her poor ability to engage in useful inferential thinking that made her conclude she should cultivate a constant conscious and literal prayed acknowledgment of gratitude to God. Her intolerance of uncertainty drove her to select a compulsion that would eliminate doubt by forcing her to do something literally and perfectly so there could be no room for doubt that she was not following the scripture. Her OCD also pushed her to perfect the moment before moving to the next one, which resulted in behavioral freezing while she verified her gratitude and acknowledgement of God's magnificence.

Often those with religious scrupulosity completely ignore issues of practicality when trying to interpret and implement religious practice because they want to eliminate doubt. Unlike their non-OCD counterparts, they ignore the impracticality of gaining certainty through perfect thought and action. Those who do not have OCD *learn to accept doubt, as opposed to eliminate doubt.* They adjust their interpretation of the religious rules to fit what is reasonably possible instead of trying to obtain perfection for the sake of eliminating doubt. For those who are scrupulous, the only way to eliminate doubt is to attain perfection in thought, action or intention, which of course is humanly impossible.

The folly of following extreme examples of sainthood

Intolerance of uncertainty drives scrupulous patients to create and observe religious rules more than the average member of their faith community would do. Scrupulous patients may also attempt to gain certainty by outperforming others in religious observance so they can verify they must have done enough by being the "best." When the patient compulsively attempts to outperform the average person, it can lead to justifying compulsions by comparison to historical religious figures who did extreme things to demonstrate faith, such as starvation or meditating for months in a cave without sustenance or human contact. Unfortunately, there are real examples of saints and revered religious authorities who have themselves suffered from scrupulosity, such as St Ignatius Loyola, the founder of the Jesuits, and Martin Luther, the founder of the Protestant Reformation (Ciarrocchi, 1995). Many religions also have exemplars or saints who have done extreme forms of fasting, self-denial, meditation and self-neglect. Children and teens who undergo religious training may learn about these exemplars. Patients who are scrupulous are at higher risk for assuming they too must follow in the footsteps of these exemplars or saints, despite the impracticality or impossibility of doing so. Those who do not have scrupulosity react to these stories as a source of inspiration for what might be possible while rejecting the notion that they should literally think and act the same way. Scrupulous patients forget that these saints and examples are rare and mistake them for a suitable role model for an average person of faith. They overlook the obvious fact that the vast majority of the faithful live, think and act as ordinary people without showing exceptional signs of supernatural religious fervor and abilities. I use the analogy with my patients of the absurdity of every human who can run assuming they will win an Olympic gold medal for being the fastest human being. Only a very few people can become the fastest human being and likewise only a very few people can become extraordinary saints.

Many scrupulous patients will be caught in the trap of trying to obtain certainty of belief, conviction or intention. Their obsessions will center around determining whether they have made a true commitment to God, a true commitment to religious observance or if they feel a true belief in aspects of their faith. They will get stuck on what it means to think or feel normal human doubt about things that are matters of opinion and experience. They might want proof they will be reincarnated into a better existence and doubt the meaning and hope of their current life. They might want proof of salvation or an afterlife. When this happens, it is difficult to manage because the patient's OCD perspective is intolerant of doubt and assumes there must be a perfect and pure way to feel, think or act that will in turn eliminate all doubt. The best way to deal with this mistaken assumption is to try the following exercises. Many patients with this intolerance of uncertainty will believe that any interruption in thinking means they must start over until they can get it perfectly right.

Exercises for patients who believe they should have perfect pure thoughts or feelings

1. Instruct the patient to focus on only purple elephants eating pink ice-cream for three minutes. Tell them they cannot think about anything else for the next three minutes and ask them to raise their hand each time they accidentally think of anything besides a purple elephant eating pink ice-cream. Set a timer and keep encouraging them to keep their thoughts perfectly on purple elephants with pink ice-cream. Keep a tally of stray thoughts and then ask the patient, "What does this prove about whether you can make your mind think only one thing? Do you think you could think of only one thing if it were about something besides purple elephants? If so, let's try again. Now, let's try doing this exposure practice using your thoughts. So, if you cannot perfectly keep your mind on something, do you think God really wants you to do something that is impossible?"

2. Instruct the patient to take a poll of other adults and peers who they believe to be good members of their faith community, to see if they can make their minds only think about one thing, or

if they can make their minds only think about God, or prayer, and so on, without letting their minds wander. You can have the patient do this during the session by texting others or have them do it as home practice. When they get the inevitable result that no one can keep their mind from wandering, ask them, "So, do you think your OCD is lying to you about how much you, or anyone, can control your mind? What can you say back to your OCD when it tries to trick you into believing you must make your thoughts/prayers/observance perfect without ever wandering to other thoughts?"

3. Instruct the patient to take a poll from their clergy and other respected members of their faith community to ask them if they ever believe they must restart their prayer, devotions, meditation and so on if their thoughts get interrupted or their mind wanders. *I have yet to have someone report that they start again, unless they got interrupted at the very beginning of their religious practice, say by a phone call or doorbell.*

Additionally, scrupulous patients typically do not understand the role of the human imagination in moral decision-making. They do not understand that to make good, moral choices, humans must also be able to imagine both good and bad choices. If humans can only imagine good, then they are just automatons who lack free will. Morality is based on the concept of free will, or the ability to choose between good and evil. To help address these sticking points, you can do the following exercises:

Exercise to illustrate how people need to think both good and bad thoughts to be moral people

1. Ask the patient what the difference is between how a robot thinks and how people think. Ask them, "If you were a robot and someone programmed you to do only nice things for people, can you ever do anything bad or naughty?" After they answer, "No," robots can only do what their programmer tells them to do, say, "Now, if you are a human and someone tells you to do something nice, can you decide to do

something naughty instead? For example, if your mum tells you to stay out of your sister's room where you know she hid some candy, is it possible for you to decide to sneak into her room to see if she has any candy hidden in her desk, even though you know it is wrong?" Once the patient says, "Yes," then you reiterate that humans are different from robots because they can tell the difference between good and bad. They get to decide what they want to do. The only way they can make a good decision is if they can imagine both a good decision and a bad decision and decide what to do, instead of being like a robot who can only do what the programmer tells them to do. Then ask, "So if you are a human being who has to always be able to imagine all the good things and all the bad things, then do you think God thinks it is bad just because you get a bad thought?" You can also ask, "Are there any of the Ten Commandments that say, 'You must only think good thoughts?'" Then ask the patient, "How can you tell if someone is a good person? Is someone a good person if they do not like someone, but they share their candy with them anyway? Is someone a good person if they want to hit another kid who says mean things, but decide not to hit them?" Then you make the point that acting like a good person is about the behavior you choose even when you have angry, hurtful or ugly thoughts. It's about acting in a kind and loving way, especially when you do not feel like it.

2. Have the patient conduct a poll of people they respect in their faith community by asking them, "Do you ever get angry or mean thoughts about God? Other people? Doing good things? Do you ever wonder if God is real? If Heaven exists? If God really loves us? Do you ever wonder if none of this is real?" After the patient gets this sample of normal information, ask them, "What does this mean for the lies that OCD tells you about not being allowed to have a human mind that can imagine all the worst things possible? If God made you this way, then why would it upset God if everyone always has to be able to think about bad things in order to be able to choose good things?"

Aiming for average and merely human

Since intolerance of uncertainty drives most scrupulous patients to attempt exceptional thought and behavioral self-control, it is helpful to define what their faith community expects of the average person and how their faith community addresses the imperfection of being human. I want the patient to have a clear idea of what the messy middle looks like for the average person who is faithful rather than getting stuck on what the extraordinary saints or egregious sinners are like. All major world religions have holy scriptures that indicate God's love and forgiveness of human limitation. This is helpful to know, because often scrupulous patients will be stuck obsessing about unforgivable sins that are poorly defined or not defined at all, permanent rejection by God, inability to obtain God's favor or inability to show sufficient faith and devotion. These are matters the average person of faith would overlook because they can tolerate doubt and assume they are in good standing.

Scrupulous patients, on the other hand, get stuck in an endless loop of reassurance seeking and checking that can take many forms. The most common is getting caught in mental self-scrutiny for purity of thought, intention and emotion while doing religious practices. For example, a patient may need to perfectly concentrate while saying prayers, when touching the Torah, while worshipping or meditating. Patients who get thought interruptions, whose intrusive thoughts seem inappropriate or who feel angry because of the burden of their OCD misunderstand the normalcy of these thought interruptions. The problem for the patient then becomes one of understanding how the mind works and how to become aware of the ways in which OCD plays against normal human ambivalence, uncertainty, shifting thoughts and shifting emotions.

Here is how I explain this to patients:

Therapist: "An attitude is an idea that you agree to with your thoughts. For example, let's say you like candy. If you like candy, it means you think pleasant thoughts about candy, you like to eat candy when you have the opportunity and you might try to persuade your parents to buy you sweets. Your attitude is the way you think about candy. Do you lose your attitude about candy on the days you do not eat candy? Do you lose your attitude about candy if you have no pocket money to buy candy? Do you hate candy just because you cannot eat it at every meal?

"An attitude about your faith is just like an attitude about candy. You do not have to be thinking about God or doing something to show you are faithful to have a good attitude about God. All you must do to have an attitude is to agree with the ideas that are important about God. The behaviors you do might show others what attitude you have, but it does not prove your attitude. You only must agree with the ideas about God even if you do not show them or think them or feel them all the time."

Normalize human ambivalence

I had one patient, Jonas, whose scrupulosity illustrated the typical way OCD can take one detail of religious practice and distort its significance, inflating it into the single most important aspect of faith. Jonas, in effect, created a religion of one that no longer reflected the values of his faith community. This always occurs when scrupulosity invades religious practice. OCD always takes guidelines and rules for religious thought and behavior out of context, distorting them and turning them into a lifestyle that is impossible to follow. OCD never focuses on the good in the patient, the good that can occur because of one's faith or the hope that a healthy faith imparts. It always ends up judging the patient as sinful, cast out, shamed or unworthy. The irony is that all major faith traditions have scriptures that make clear humans are worthy of God's attention, love and forgiveness. The following case example describes how to assist patients like Jonas to discern between distortions of faith and true religion as practiced by the average believer. Pointing out how a patient's scrupulosity requires inhuman levels of concentration, devotion or perfection for things that can never be controlled, such as imagination or mood, can be profoundly helpful. Anxiety and intolerance of uncertainty makes scrupulous patients overlook the deviations their OCD religion of one has created. Consider the example of Lucy.

CASE EXAMPLE

Lucy was a 16-year-old whose scrupulosity took root during her confirmation classes for her Catholic church. She had attended Catholic schools and heard many stories of the lives of saints, some of which detailed extreme levels of fasting, self-denial and ability to endure human suffering. Her confirmation classes emphasized the seriousness of making a commitment to the church, which inspired Lucy to take up fasting and self-denial to demonstrate her sincerity of faith. She wanted to emulate St Teresa of Calcutta, who had lived and worked with the poor in India during the 20th century. She knew St Teresa ate the same food as her invalid patients, slept on the floor or a rough cot and considered it her duty to welcome the suffering that went with working with the dying and indigent. Lucy began by refusing sweet and junk food to renounce what she considered luxurious foods. Next, she felt feeling full was gluttonous and began only eating until not quite full. She also began praying with her rosary for the poor and dying each night. If she failed to concentrate properly, she had to repeat her prayers until there were no mistakes. Her OCD made her believe that lack of concentration equaled lack of sincerity because she was so privileged and well fed and should give her best efforts in prayer for those less fortunate. Then she began to fast from one meal a day to show her willingness to suffer with the poor. She began praying late into the night until she was sleep deprived, sometimes falling asleep on her knees in prayer. Her parents noticed she had bruises on her knees and began to question her devotion. When she gave away all her birthday gifts to the poor, her parents became concerned and consulted the parish priest.

Her parish priest recognized Lucy had scrupulosity and instructed her family to seek mental health treatment. He also told her that not everyone is called to sainthood, hoping to help her let go of her compulsions. She prayed about this idea and believed she was indeed called to sainthood because she said she felt such peace, knowing she was doing the right thing to honor God. She then stopped eating any complete meals and only drank water and ate very small bowls of rice, such as the poor in the slums of Calcutta might eat. Discussion with Lucy revealed she was mistaking the decrease in anxiety that came with deciding to do something more rigorous to appease her OCD as a sign from God to be saintlier. She saw her bruised knees as a sign of devotion and willingness to share in Christ's suffering. She also admitted she had been sleeping on the floor of her bedroom with no blankets for the same reason. She was able to admit that her compulsions were outside the norm for other Catholics but misinterpreted her feeling of decreased anxiety as God's sign she was called to extreme self-denial. Here is how I worked with Lucy to help her identify OCD as her enemy and not an unwillingness to be called by God to sainthood.

I obtained permission to consult with her priest and parents to find out what had been said to Lucy about sainthood. I verified that although the members of her confirmation class had been encouraged to consider occasional short fasts—such as missing lunch at school and giving the money that would have been spent on lunch to the needy—no one had been encouraged to do the kinds of things Lucy did. The priest had, in fact, indicated that this sort of extreme religious practice was a rare example of sainthood and church policy was to avoid things that risked self-harm or interfered with healthy living. He also verified that others who are considered wise and experienced in religious practice must confirm whether someone is called to a vocation, such as the priesthood. Thus, someone cannot self-appoint into a special category of behavior or practice. Simply feeling convinced is not enough to receive a special calling in the church. Similarly, the human body is sacred. Doing things that deprive a person of sleep, cause bruising or interfere with good health and the tasks of daily living such as school or chores, is wrong.

Armed with this knowledge, I arranged a meeting with Lucy and her priest to help her see how her OCD was pulling her away from a true faith and leading her in the direction of contradicting God and church tradition. Being able to establish this concept often makes it much easier for the patient to agree to treatment and to label their symptoms as OCD. I did two things; first, I used Socratic questioning to help Lucy see that her good intention was to be a good Catholic, then to establish the boundaries for being a good Catholic as defined by an agreed-on religious authority and finally to see how her symptoms fitted criteria for OCD rather than religious devotion attainable by any average human. Second, I verified that the priest understood scrupulosity and the long tradition of the Catholic church of prescribing abstinence from compulsions as the proper treatment for scrupulosity OCD.

My questions were the following:

1. What is the purpose of prayer, fasting and other acts of devotion?

2. How does the church know that someone is called to a special vocation or calling, such as being a priest, a nun or a monk who will engage in special and more demanding acts of deprivation?

3. What kinds of things does the church think is wrong for special acts of devotion, even if someone feels they have received a special calling?

4. Can people do things to guarantee that they become canonized as a saint? Can people control what God does with their thoughts, feelings or behavior?

5. Does the church recognize OCD as a problem that can interfere with how someone thinks about God or the way they believe they must think, feel or act?

6. What does the church say people should do when they have scrupulosity OCD?

After asking these questions, I then wrote the patient's symptoms on a dry erase board and beside these the characteristics of OCD and asked her to see if any of her obsessions and compulsions matched the symptoms of OCD, which she recognized. Here is an example:

My thoughts and behaviors	What is typical of OCD
When I think about trying to be saintly, I always feel anxious	The thought makes me feel doubt, uncertainty, anxiety and dread
The more I talk to people and try to remember what I read, said and did, the more my thoughts get unclear	I feel more confused the more I try to figure it out
Even though I have given up a lot, I feel anxious, tired and worried	My thoughts always end up with me not being good enough or trying hard enough
I feel good for a little bit each time I vow to serve God better, but then that feeling always goes away	Even if I do feel certain for a moment, it is because I committed to doing something even stricter, purer or with more dedication
I feel more worried about fasting, self-indulgence and being saintly, even though I do so much more than other people	I keep cycling back and must go through the same cycle of thoughts, doubts, uncertainty and try to get it right

After creating this chart, I ask Lucy and her priest an important question: "What is supposed to be the outcome of living a good or holy life? How do people feel, including the formal saints, who achieve a good life?" Each of the four major world religions has the same answer. Good living or holy living always leads to joy, peace and better-quality relationships with others. It never leads to bruised knees, irritability, anxiety, increased intolerance of uncertainty, poor performance or misery. The conscience of the righteous person is light because they know they are living well and experiencing the benefits of good living. Anxiety, doubt, compulsion and repetitive cycles of guilt, shame and doubt are never the outcome of true good living. I asked Lucy's priest to tell me how history describes the lives of the saints, how they felt about their lives, their relationship with God and with others. The answer is they felt bliss, self-confidence, unwavering faith, and commitment to their life as a Christian.

They were able to feel joy even when suffering. Next, I asked the patient, "What do people feel like when they live a life full of OCD? How come they end up in treatment?" The answer that everyone gets right is something like, "OCD makes people miserable. It ruins everything with anxiety, intrusive thoughts and compulsions. Kids with OCD do not come to my office because they are full of peace, love, joy and lots of lovely relationships." Lastly, I asked Lucy, "Now, can you tell me which side your thoughts about God, holy living and trying to do the right thing reflect? Do they reflect the torture of OCD, or do they sound like true messages from God meant to make you feel closer to God and closer to other people and have more peace and joy in your heart and mind?" Once we finished this comparison, Lucy agreed that her OCD was unreasonable and never kind. She also agreed that God was kind and wanted good things for her. She was much more willing to engage in ERP and I used this touchpoint throughout therapy by asking her, "Is what you think you should do something that will lead to feeling peace, joy and love or is it just to get rid of anxiety?" Obtaining this moment of insight can be very helpful for setting the stage for exposure practice. The patient understands the requirement to go against their OCD during treatment. It no longer feels like a terrible compromise of faith. Their desire to avoid or do compulsions may wax and wane according to anxiety, but they will have a mental grasp of the rationale for treatment which creates a wedge between their intrusive thoughts and submission to the demands of their intrusive thoughts.

Is the problem fear of uncertainty, fear of a bad outcome or both?

Determining the source of the patient's anxiety is important for determining how to conduct imaginal (in the mind) and in vivo (in real life) exposure with response prevention. Some patients will focus on avoiding disgrace, losing salvation with God, going to Hell, or being excluded from the faith community. When this occurs, the idea of alienation from God, the community, or being doomed to a poor-quality afterlife becomes prominent and often leads to avoidance of thinking about these topics, or mention of these topics. Compulsions will focus on doing things that undo feared thoughts or images, that secure a good outcome, such as praying compulsively, repeatedly asking for forgiveness or confessing belief in Jesus, God or performing rituals designed to offset bad karma. When this occurs, it is important to target the feared ideas while fading back or stopping the compulsive avoidance and/or rituals the patient uses to secure certainty toward a good outcome. Imaginal exposure can be a useful tool for taking away the power of intrusive thoughts and making it easier to do any necessary in vivo exposure. Let me explain with the example of Roger.

CASE EXAMPLE

Roger was an eight-year-old whose parents regarded his initial prayers for everyone in his family to be saved by Jesus as charming until he began asking them repeatedly if he and his entire family were going to Heaven, person by person. He refused to wear, eat or touch anything red, which was a problem because his school colors contained red. His OCD would say things such as, "You looked at red. You must love the Devil. You are going to Hell!" or, "What if you are going to Hell and everyone else goes to Heaven?" He also avoided anything that began with a "D" because this referred to the Devil. His parents also noticed him repeatedly pausing during play, bowing his head and muttering something to himself. He would not reveal what he was doing other than to say, "Stop interrupting me! I am talking to Jesus!"

Treatment began with imaginal exposure since Roger thought this was an easier first step than doing things like looking at red, touching red or eating red. We also had his priest explain to him that because he was baptized and wanted to love Jesus, even though no one can perfectly love Jesus, he was only going to go to Heaven. The priest also explained that sometimes he talked about Hell to help the people who don't want to love Jesus and that these messages were not meant for boys who were baptized Christians. His parents were instructed to not use this information as a reassurance tool when Roger was anxious, but instead to use it in non-anxious discussion about being Christian during family prayer or family worship.

His imaginal exposure went like this: "Roger, I want you to repeat after me. I am going to say words and things that will make your OCD get scared. Remember, we are trying to scare your OCD so you can stop it from beating you up by convincing you that you are going to the bad place." I refrained from saying "Hell" because this was very challenging for him early in treatment. "So, let's get started by whispering. Repeat after me. D, D, D, D, now, your turn." We did this until he could do it louder and at a normal volume. "Dev, Dev, Dev, Dev, Dev, now, your turn." I also had him draw half of a letter "D" repeatedly while saying the sound of the letter "D" so he had to both look at, say and hear the dreaded sounds. Then we repeated the word, "eevull" to mimic the later sounds of the word devil. We drew devil horns, first part way and then completely, then added colors, such as black and then red. We progressed to saying the word, "Devil," first at a whisper and then repeatedly until he could do it at normal volume. I also had his parents repeat the same sounds and words. Once Roger could say, "Devil," we began using the same technique for "Hell" and used the word, "H, E, double hockey sticks" as part of the progression to being able to say the word "Hell." I also had him draw pictures of Hell, which he put up in his bedroom and house alongside pictures of the Devil.

Subsequent sessions added in phrases, beginning with indefinite statements, "What if someone goes to Hell?" followed by, "What if a boy goes to Hell?" then, "What if I go to Hell?" and lastly "I am going to go to Hell!" and his parents and I saying, "Sorry Roger, but you are going to Hell. So glad it is not me." Response prevention focused on banning all reassurance seeking with prayer, silent prayer and avoiding things that had become exposure practice. His parents decided that it would be better to temporarily refrain from bedtime prayer until his OCD symptoms improved. Once he easily tolerated wearing, eating and looking at red things, words beginning with the letter D, and stopped seeking reassurance, we added in bedtime prayer with a final phrase, "And I hope that none of this is true and I go to Hell forever!" His in vivo exposure consisted of putting in plain view things that were red, had the letter D, pictures of the Devil, wearing a Devil costume, watching age-appropriate cartoons featuring a Devil character and watching the movie trailers that triggered the initial symptoms.

Extreme observance

Some patients will be caught up in extreme observance without necessarily being concerned about eternal outcomes. Their focus will be on avoiding the shame that comes from imperfect implementation of the rules for dress, eating and so on. They will also suffer from intolerance of uncertainty as it applies to following the rules. In these cases, obtaining clear guidelines for proper observance and clear guidance for implementing exposure with response prevention is important. Compulsions will often revolve around seeking reassurance by questioning others and religious authorities on the proper way to follow rules for observance. Other compulsions will revolve around implementing an ever-stricter version of the rules to make sure the bare minimum of the rule is accurately followed. For example, a Muslim girl was brought to my clinic because she kept bruising her skin by pulling her hijab too tightly and had headaches from doing so. She also repeatedly asked others if any hair was showing beneath her hijab. She was trying to make sure that no hair escaped the boundaries of her head scarf. Similarly, a teenage Buddhist girl began avoiding eating any foods she could not verify were completely vegetarian for fear of violating the rule of non-harm. She became fearful that food might be contaminated with animal parts or insect parts and refused to eat anything packaged or prepared out of her sight. She also repeatedly scanned her seat before sitting down, or the ground before stepping, and became very slow at moving anywhere due to exercising extreme caution about not accidentally squashing microscopic baby bugs. She repeatedly asked for reassurance from others to verify she had done no harm.

Each of these patients illustrates going beyond what is required for normal observance and the way OCD creates guidelines much stricter than those required of others in their faith community. The following is an example of how I worked with the teenage boy who feared inappropriate eye gaze.

CASE EXAMPLE

Jakob was 12 when he first noticed that he felt sensations of sexual attraction to females when thinking about them or being near them. He had followed his orthodox Jewish community's rules for remaining separate from females and never questioned his observance until he realized he was feeling attracted to females. He then surmised he should be more careful to avoid creating sexual thoughts so he could follow his community's injunction to avoid such thoughts. He consulted his father and other men who all explained that he should follow the rules to avoid looking at women and to avoid sexual arousal to remain modest. Jakob's parents initially viewed his behaviors as being modest and appropriate though they saw they were an exaggeration of what teens did. When Jakob's apparent modesty began to include keeping his eyes down when around his mother and sisters, his parents became concerned. Jakob also misunderstood his adolescent development of sexual arousal and sexual curiosity as being immodest. By the time his parents sought treatment, he was unable to look up unless he was in an all-male setting, and he avoided being in the presence of all females. He also refused to attend many of the important celebrations that included both genders, such as bar mitzvahs and weddings. In the past, he would have attended these events and hung out with the males during the festivities. His rabbi had referred him for treatment. He attended treatment with me, a female, only because his rabbi had instructed him to do so.

Prior to meeting Jakob and his parents, I made sure to wear modest dress that covered my arms, legs, neckline and included a skirt with dark stockings. I did this to make it easier for his family to attend treatment and avoid unnecessary discomfort. I also refrained from shaking the father's hand and requested that both parents attend treatment so there would not be the awkwardness of two men being alone with an unknown woman. If only Jakob's father had attended, I would have had to leave my office door partly open to avoid any appearance of immodesty. I was worried this might inhibit Jakob from speaking as freely as possible during treatment.

When I met Jakob, he faced away from me and refused to answer my initial questions. His father showed normal modest observant behavior by not looking directly at me and refraining from shaking my hand in greeting. He did, however, look at my face while I spoke and looked away when it was not necessary. I noticed that Jakob's hands were red and chapped and I discovered that he was also washing more than is required prior to prayer, which is just a simple rinsing with water. I discovered Jakob doubted whether he had properly rinsed his hands and repeated the rinsing until it felt right, or until he felt sure his entire hand and wrist were thoroughly wet. He also repeatedly wrung his hands together to make sure they felt right. Private discussion with the parents revealed they also suspected Jakob was taking cold showers to try and get rid of sexual feelings, since he would exit the bathroom with visible goosebumps and appeared to be cold.

My consultation with the rabbi was a delicate one, since I was trying to find out which matters of adolescent sexuality were permissible for discussion and which were not. I learned that masturbation and any deliberate focus on sexual thought were forbidden, though it was accepted that the yetzer hara, or inclination toward evil, could result in spontaneous sexual thoughts and feelings. Jewish men were not to have ejaculations outside marriage, though nocturnal emissions are understood to be involuntary and therefore not something that qualifies as bad. Were a man to masturbate and ejaculate, he should take a ritual cleansing bath, a mikvah. The proper response to sexual urges and feelings outside marriage is to ignore them. I also learned that sex education does not occur until someone is ready to marry. I got the rabbi's consent to explain that the sexual thoughts and feelings Jakob was experiencing were the normal growth of his body in preparation for marriage and therefore not something to be ashamed of. I explained to the rabbi how Jakob's attempts at thought suppression would only make him think more inappropriate thoughts. I explained how the negative reinforcement of avoiding spontaneous sexual feelings and images while in the presence of women would only get worse because of Jakob's OCD. I gave examples of how I handled this type of exposure with non-orthodox teens by having the patient recall feared sexual thoughts, and I asked for his help designing appropriate exposure with response prevention.

The rabbi consulted with several other rabbis and gave me this guideline. Under no circumstances could I suggest any new sexual thoughts or images. I should have the father present to conduct all treatment that focused on Jakob's eye gaze so the father could give instruction to reduce any spontaneous threat should I make a mistake in implementing ERP. Jakob could be asked to notice, allow and then ignore his feared thoughts without trying to think of any new thoughts. The rabbi and Jakob's father also agreed to normalize the adolescent experience of sexual thoughts and urges. I was allowed to talk about how OCD made him do more than was necessary and how the Torah and Talmud made allowances for him by setting up rules that did not need to be improved on. He was to strictly avoid any embellishments of observance and to avoid pornography. We agreed that Jakob would be allowed to face me, to look in my direction and to look at my face while I spoke and the same would be true for other women who were well known to him, such as female family members. He was permitted to hold his eye gaze, so he could travel in a room or crowd while also avoiding directly looking at females when it was not necessary to do so. The rabbi also told me that three seconds for both hands under a running tap would be sufficient for a ritual handwashing prior to prayer.

Subsequently, I conducted exposure practice with Jakob in the following manner, illustrated below. I instructed him to notice, allow and then let go of any upsetting thoughts while focusing on the exposure task, I asked him to raise his hand if he got an intrusive thought so I could keep track of what was happening during exposure. If he raised his hand, I praised him for fighting back against his OCD and instructed him to notice the thought while letting go of it and then to return to the task. I used the concept of Jakob's OCD taking away his ability to choose which thoughts to pay attention to and used the exposure practice to learn how to choose which thoughts to focus on. These are the tasks he completed:

1. Briefly turning his torso toward me with eyes closed, then increasing duration of turning with eyes closed.

2. Briefly opening eyes while turning torso toward me and looking at his feet for one second, then two, then three, and so on, until he could keep his eyes open.

3. Briefly turning toward me with eyes looking at his shoes, then naming three things he saw on the floor from a selection which I had laid out near his feet. I laid objects closer to me and his mother and repeated the exercise.

4. Sitting facing one quarter toward me while doing the previous tasks.

5. Sitting half facing me and his mother while doing the previous tasks.

6. Sitting fully facing me and his mother while doing the previous tasks.

7. Sitting facing me and describing the shoes I and his mother were wearing.

8. Looking briefly at my hands and telling me what object I was holding. Doing the same with his mother.

9. Reading a sign I was holding in my hands.

10. Looking briefly at me and telling me what I was wearing. I put on a series of silly hats or silly items, such as Mardi Gras beads, on my head.

11. Doing steps 4–10 with other female staff and then with his sisters at home.

12. Walking through busy areas such as shops and cafes while having to describe to me what color clothing women wore, what type of shoes they wore and what items were in his surroundings. I would ask him, "Tell me the names of five drinks on the menu behind the barista in the coffee shop." He had to do the same type of exposure practice in his home community.

Jakob was able to progress through treatment and no longer appear to be staring at the ground while near women. He was able to practice brief ritual handwashing at the sink in my office, where we timed three seconds until he could do it without me counting down and cutting off the water. He followed the same handwashing practice at home until he could do it on his own without his father having to turn off the water or count the time. Much of the success of his treatment was due to the help the rabbi provided with designing exposure with response prevention, along with Jakob's willingness to accept the rabbi's religious authority to tell Jakob he should cooperate with treatment.

If you are unfamiliar with the basic precepts of morality with major religions, it is helpful to review some basic theological principles so you can know how to approach motivating and engaging your patient in treatment. The Resources section in the back of this book summarizes five major religions, Christianity, Judaism, Islam, Buddhism and Hinduism, so you have a quick reference if you are unfamiliar with the general tenets of each faith.

Next, I will discuss treatment of scrupulosity as it occurs outside a religious context.

(If you would like to view a demonstration of how to implement some of the strategies mentioned in this chapter, please go to https://library.jkp.com/redeem using the code ZVEAZDD.

CHAPTER 5

Treating Scrupulosity OCD

Social Justice, Climate Change and Morality
Obsessions and Compulsions

Author's note: For the purposes of clarity, this chapter will use the term morality-based OCD to refer to non-religion-based scrupulosity while acknowledging that all religion-based scrupulosity also focuses on morality. Any variant of OCD scrupulosity focuses on morality. Although the basic treatment techniques are the same for all types of scrupulosity, clinical experience has shown me that morality-based scrupulosity has nuances in clinical care that are separate from religion-based scrupulosity. Thus, the distinction between this chapter and the previous chapter.

How morality-based scrupulosity is different from religion-based scrupulosity

Many patients suffer from OCD that revolves around ethical dilemmas of living that are often misunderstood or overlooked as the result of OCD. Scrupulous obsessions and compulsions can manifest in concerns about global warming, social justice, veganism, animal rights, socialism and extreme morality focused on telling the truth and more. In this instance, OCD hijacks common cultural concerns about morality that are independent of organized religion. Just as with religion-based OCD, scrupulosity about other concerns is not caused by the situation, but rather OCD co-opts the situation and gets stuck on matters that have to do with opinion, nuances of morality and variations in expression of moral behaviors. What further complicates this subtype of OCD is a lack of common agreed application of ideals and moral values because it is not an organized community with agreed on standards, but rather a loose collection of people who share similar values. For example, a teen can care about animal rights and demonstrate commitment by any one of the following: being kind to a pet, volunteering at an animal shelter, signing petitions against abusive livestock practices, or adopting a vegan lifestyle that avoids use of animal products. There is no overall governing body of animal rights that prescribes the values and appropriate lifestyle for being concerned about animal rights. This creates uncertainty, which in turn makes it easy for scrupulosity to take root.

Just as in religion-based scrupulosity, there are exemplars of people who have more extreme lifestyles that any patient can point to for the sake of comparison. Patients with morality-based scrupulosity often assume stricter and more extreme behaviors are the only way to demonstrate sincerity and commitment. Since there is no agreed way to measure sincerity or commitment, OCD attempts to eliminate uncertainty by requiring progressively stricter methods of behaving to make things more certain. For example, a patient might get an intrusive thought after feeling happy that they are being cavalier in the face of global warming and then feel compelled to read grim news about climate change and avoid going places that require non-electric transportation, even when it means missing important activities. For the clinician, this can make it more difficult to set boundaries for normal behaviors and non-OCD ways to demonstrate sincerity. Since there are no agreed authorities or standards, it can be more difficult than it is when working with religion-based OCD to create reasonable standards for ERP and recovery the patient will agree with. Additionally, families may feel less compassion for the patient's scrupulous concerns because they may not see the validity of the patient's basic value of self-sacrifice or moral purity. For example, a parent of a patient who wants a vegan lifestyle may believe their child is silly and inviting malnourishment. The patient and parents can then get into a power struggle about basic values that makes it more difficult for the patient to engage in treatment. Parents also frequently view recovery as elimination of the values underlying the patient's scrupulosity rather than developing a healthy way to manage moral values. For example, I often hear parents tell me they wish their child would give up their moral focus rather then find a healthy way to express it.

Lastly, the lack of agreed standards for non-religion-based moral behaviors is so murky, it sometimes results in the patient concluding it is up to them to set and maintain the moral standard regardless of what others think and do. This can be especially challenging because attempts to use perspective taking, cognitive reframing or acceptance of uncertainty are often trumped by phrases such as these: "Someone must do this, and it might as well be me!" or, "Even if I am the only one who cares, at least I care!" or, "It's my right to choose who I am!" Learning how to address each of these issues will make your treatment more effective. I will address each of these in the following chapter.

Lack of agreed standards for non-religion-based moral behaviors is so murky, it sometimes results in the patient concluding it is up to them to set and maintain the moral standard regardless of what others think and do.

Creating a standard for healthy expression of morality

As mentioned above, the lack of agreed community standards for cultural moral issues poses a challenge for determining how healthy expression of morality might look. When setting up ERP and imaginal exposure practice, it is necessary to know what the average non-OCD person does. For example, we know that most people do not really keep their hands perfectly clean and often touch their shoes, the floor or other unclean surfaces and then eat with unclean hands without washing. So, we have contamination OCD patients touch shoes, floors and other surfaces and then lick their hands and eat finger foods without washing to mimic this normal behavior. It is easy to have a contamination OCD patient poll others about how often they really wash their hands or use public toilets without decontamination washing to get normative data. What do you do, however, when your patient is a self-declared disciple of global warming, and they refuse to ride any transportation that is not people-powered regardless of the cost to their social life, academic studies or extracurricular activities?

Although your patient can point to Greta Thunberg, an exemplar of commitment to preventing climate disaster, Greta has a family who is also committed and able to promote her chosen lifestyle of using sailboats, buses, electric cars and trains for all travel, including international travel. This would be unattainable for most patients and families. Here are the steps I use to help set an agreed standard for guiding ERP and healthy lifestyle.

Step 1: Define the basic values the patient's scrupulosity expresses. These values are typically about compassion for others, the planet, society's well-being or the unfortunate.

CASE EXAMPLE

Colleen began refusing to wear or use anything new after she read how many factories create global waste and abuse workers. She gave away all her new clothing and possessions to a thrift shop and would only wear and use items purchased second hand. She refused to use any "new" items in her home and would sit on the floor rather than use furniture. She also found food thrown into rubbish bins behind restaurants and insisted she be allowed to eat this food instead of meals prepared by her mum. We identified the values of her scrupulosity as being attempts to care for others, to prevent abuse of workers, to care for the planet and to decrease landfill.

Step 2: Define the way OCD hijacks the patient's values by attempting to eliminate uncertainty with repeated tests of sincerity, purity or adherence to OCD rules.

This is how I described the effect Colleen's OCD had on her attempts to live her values. "Colleen, it looks as if you have great compassion for others, the planet and for how industry operates in our world. I really want you to be able to be the kind of girl who has integrity and lives her values, so the world really is a better place because of you. It looks as if your OCD has accidentally taken over your good values by turning them into a set of rules that guarantees that you are the most sincere, pure and perfect girl ever to follow these rules. Does that sound like it might be true?"

Colleen: "Yes, I guess so."

Therapist: "You are right that we all need to act. It sounds as if you feel that you must compensate for everyone. That seems unfair. Isn't it right that we all need to do something and not just you? It looks as if your OCD is accidentally pushing you to always do more and never feels satisfied. Does that sound like you?"

Colleen: "I guess you are right. I just couldn't stand myself if I didn't do something. I don't want to be one of those people who just talks and complains and does nothing."

Therapist: "It seems as if your OCD must always feel certain and guaranteed that you are doing the right thing, even when you know you are already a good person. It won't let you rest. The good news is that you do not need OCD to do good things. In fact, OCD takes up so much of your thoughts and feelings that it is going to make you miserable instead of feeling that you are really accomplishing something. Isn't that right? You told me that you feel as if you never do enough."

Step 3: Discuss with the patient how self-compassion should accompany healthy morality and result in peace of mind because one is living with integrity while recognizing no one can ever attain perfection in their thinking, feelings or behaviors.

Therapist: "I noticed that compassion for all beings is one of your values. I assume that includes you, since you are also a human. Does that make sense?"

Colleen: "Yes. It's just I shouldn't live as privileged if that hurts others."

Therapist: "That is a good point. We don't want to take advantage of others. Have you thought about how every time you take a breath, you breathe in air that no one else can breathe, or you eat food or take up space no one else can use? Doesn't that mean that every person ends up affecting others and using resources that others could use no matter what? It seems as if your OCD made a rule that says you cannot do anything that affects others when that is an impossible rule to follow. Would you get mad at someone because they were not able to find any clothes they could afford that were made with no pollution, by fair wage workers and by companies that gave all their profits to prevent global warming? Would you insist others made their clothes out of rags if they could not find anything at the thrift store that fitted them?"

Colleen: "I wouldn't get mad, although I wish everyone would do more. Someone must do something. I never thought about it like that."

Therapist: "It sounds as if you can be compassionate toward others because you are willing to give them a free pass if they cannot find the least impactful clothes. Wouldn't it make sense to use the same standards for yourself? Can you think of any reason you are not worthy of the same compassion you would give a friend or stranger?

"Also, science shows us that people who follow their values with self-compassion are likely to feel inner peace of mind about both wanting to do great good and only being human and unable to ever be perfectly good. How does that sound compared to what OCD says?"

Step 4: Define and discuss the problems associated with perfectionism that include chronic lack of self-compassion, chronic feelings of failure and increased risk for depression, anxiety and suicide completion. Discuss how morality-based OCD is a form of perfectionism about morality that is impossible for any human to attain and therefore unrealistic.

Therapist: "I have been mentioning the word perfectionism a lot. Do you know what I mean and what we know about what perfectionism does to your mental health?"

Colleen: "Isn't that when you do things really well?"

Therapist: "Perfectionism is where you insist there is only one perfect way to do things and believe mistakes are catastrophes instead of learning opportunities. Kids who are perfectionists always feel like a failure just for being normal and making normal mistakes and not doing things just right. When you won't allow yourself to be anything less than perfect, you make it really easy for OCD to pummel you for not being absolutely perfect, even though it is impossible for humans to be perfect. OCD like yours is like super-charged perfectionism."

Colleen: "So what am I supposed to do?"

Therapist: "This is where exposure with response prevention can help you find the messy middle ground for being a good person who lives their values without being miserable with anxiety and doubt."

Step 5: Find other areas of morality in which the patient is realistic and practical because of compassion and self-compassion. Use these as an example of setting realistic goals. For example, if the patient is willing to tell a white lie to avoid hurting someone's feelings even though they believe honesty is important, then they are accepting that total honesty is not practical or kind in certain circumstances. How might they apply this idea to their OCD? For example, might they aim to earn enough money as an adult to purchase an electric car rather than miss out on friends' parties or gatherings because only a car can get them to the location and it is impossible for their parents to purchase an electric car?

Therapist: "I noticed that your OCD does not bother you about what you eat. You appear to enjoy the candy in my office, and I have heard you ask your mum to go out for fast food after we meet, even though it is likely that the workers who made the candy and food you ate were underpaid and working in unpleasant conditions. What is your non-OCD mind telling you about how it is okay to eat candy and fast food compared to what your OCD would say if it was worried about everything you ate?"

Colleen: "Well, I like sweets and chips! I would hate it if my OCD told me I was not allowed to eat them."

Therapist: "I don't know if you have realized this, but your healthy non-OCD mind says it's okay to do some things just for fun, just because it makes you happy, right?"

Colleen: "Right."

Therapist: "That's right! Teens who are good people allow themselves to do some things that are fun even when they know things are not perfect. They give themselves good credit for making sure they do some things, and not all things, that are good and help others. They let go of not being able to make things perfect. This is what we have to teach you so you can push back against your OCD."

Step 6: Set up a continuum of morality from practical and kind to perfect and unkind to self and others. Draw this on a paper or whiteboard to illustrate the continuum of choices and tell the patient the goal is to live somewhere in the middle zone to avoid both moral sloppiness and OCD perfection that is unkind.

Therapist: "Let's make it easier to see how many good choices you can make to be a good person who helps others and the planet. On one side, we will have things that selfish and uncaring people do and on the other side the things that OCD makes you do. Once you catch on, I want you to help me fill in the middle and that will be where we will focus our exposure and response prevention practice."

Refuse to believe in global warming or that workers
are abused, and change nothing

Ignore the news and buy name brands

Recycle and upcycle, use public transportation
whenever possible, turn out the lights

Do clothing swaps with friends, use thrift stores, find
affordable fair trade, combine car trips

Combine affordable new and thrift clothing, recycle,
upcycle and ride a bike instead of the bus

Go to protests, buy fair trade when possible, wear second hand clothes

Buy only from thrift stores but wear gifts that are new, but
tell others to give you only second hand things

Buy only at thrift stores, tell everyone you know about abused workers

Sew your own clothes out of rags, only purchase fair trade items at thrift stores

Helping parents

As mentioned earlier, parents of young people with morality-based scrupulosity may accidentally overlook the core values expressed in their scrupulous obsessions and compulsions. They may dismiss the healthy part of the patient's values, which often cultivates a power struggle between the patient and parent. For example, parents might consider a vegan diet to be inadequate nutrition and have the goal of eliminating it as opposed to helping the patient eat a nutritious vegan diet. Parents might prefer the convenience of a car to using public transportation or consider riding a bike to school to be a dangerous activity. They might feel comfortable lying to make excuses for non-attendance at work or consider it okay to collect unreported cash payments to avoid taxes. Each of these situations might cause problems when helping the patient set a messy middle zone for moral behavior that goes against OCD when the parents' initial response is to disagree. Additionally, most parents have the goal of passing along their moral values to their children. They often fail to remember that most adolescents and emerging adults find their own variations on the morality of their family of origin. I handle these situations by identifying and naming the power struggle, empathizing with everyone's point of view, and subsequently trying to help the family shift into a mutual struggle against OCD. I try to pitch the concept that OCD is pitting them against each other. My conversation with the family might go like this:

Therapist: "It looks as if you have all been getting really angry and resentful with each other about what OCD has been doing to your Jack. It must be horribly frustrating. Jack, I can see, too, that you feel as if no one cares about being honest or telling the truth because your parents raised you to be truthful and then got mad at you for letting your class know your parents took a bunch of cash under the table at their restaurant. Mum and Dad, I can see how betrayed and hurt you feel that Jack told others about this because this money has paid for his schooling and sports. You might even be scared that someone will tell the authorities. What really worries me, though, is how Jack's

OCD has pitted you against each other and convinced everyone to fight with each other instead of against OCD. Can we all agree that we wouldn't be here unless Jack had OCD? (Everyone gives head nods.) The big problem is how to help Jack overcome his OCD. We cannot do that so long as Jack believes you don't want him to be a good person, and Mum and Dad, so long as you believe Jack is disrespectful, ungrateful and trying to send you to prison. Wouldn't it be better to work together to get rid of the problem of OCD rather than get stuck in hurt feelings about what family members mean with their behavior? The real enemy is OCD."

Setting up exposure practice

Exposure practice for morality is like the ERP for religion-based scrupulosity as described in Chapter 4. There are the same issues of intolerance of uncertainty and fear of a bad outcome, which in this case is shame for misperceived moral failing. Less frequently, patients may also fear shaming themselves in front of others when they are part of a larger community which shares their values, such as a social media group for veganism or animal rights. It will be important to ascertain which things trigger the patient's OCD so that you can set up the previously described continuum of morality to use for designing exposure practices. It is also important to continually remind the patient that they are practicing addressing their fear of uncertainty, doubt, bad outcome or shame so they learn that their practice is about building emotional and mental resilience rather than just doing a list of difficult things. Both imaginal exposure that addresses feared ideas, images and scenarios and in vivo exposure practice with the necessary response prevention will work well. The following is an example of first imaginal exposure and then in vivo exposure practice with response prevention.

CASE EXAMPLE

Parvati was a teen who began turning all the lights off after learning about the effects of energy use on global warming. She became anxious and irritable if someone did not immediately turn off the lights and began using fewer lights during the evening to do her schoolwork, enough so that her parents worried she would strain her eyes. She refused to use any light that was not a high-efficiency LED bulb and annoyed family members by unscrewing lightbulbs in fixtures she deemed unnecessary. She began refusing to be transported in a car, preferring to walk or bike. Her mother considered this to be dangerous because some of the routes to her school and friends' homes had heavy traffic or went through neighborhoods the mother believed unsafe. Parvati had fought with her parents after sneaking in bike rides through these forbidden areas. She began having difficulty completing school assignments that required research because she rationed the number of charges to her laptop and smartphone to three per week. She set a goal to use no plastics that in turn meant she could no longer use digital devices or many items at home, school or in public, at which point her parents brought her into treatment.

Parvati was ambivalent about treatment because she felt morally compelled to compensate for the harmful effects on the climate that she saw her family and community create. She agreed she was anxious, irritable and compulsive but saw no other choices for expressing her morality. Her mother's anxious perception of dangerous neighborhoods and traffic was exaggerated. After getting her mother to agree that she herself had walked and ridden her bike everywhere without parental supervision at the same age as the patient, I persuaded her mother to take comfort in her daughter's independence and willingness to take positive moral action that reduced the burden of driving for the mother. I also pointed out that her daughter had a history of being cautious and would likely continue to be that way since she came from an extended family with lots of anxiety disorders and a fear of risk taking.

Imaginal exposure began with repeating feared statements that reflected both bad outcome and uncertainty. They are illustrated below:

Exposure statement/story	Response prevention
What if I do not do enough?	Do nothing in response to statements
What if I am the only one who can do something to save the planet?	Avoid reading about global warming, avoid talking about global warming
What if the planet dies before I do?	Avoid seeking reassurance by seeing what global warming activists are doing
I feel I will watch all life die because I helped the planet get too polluted and too hot to sustain life	Do all of the above

Once Parvati became more tolerant of her intrusive thoughts, we began in vivo exposure with response prevention practice. We set up a rule for her parents to not ask about her walking or biking, but only to insist that she attend all important events in a timely fashion, including having to ride in a car with the family when that was necessary. Here are examples of her in vivo exposure practice:

Exposure practice	Response prevention
Sit in parents' car and turn the engine on and off	Do not compensate by avoiding cars
Read articles about people who do not believe in global warming	Say, "I agree with this" and do not refute in the mind
Leave shopping bags at home and request plastic bags at the stores, buy plastic wrapped items, use plastic hangers, wear plastic foam shoes	Do not seek reassurance by looking up news about reduction of plastics
Turn on all the lights in the bedroom while in that room	Do not dim the lights or turn off others' lights
Turn on all the lights in the house	Do not remind others to turn off the lights
Use digital devices for a complete assignment or texting conversation while the device is still charging	Stop counting the number of charges on digital devices, leave devices plugged in after they are charged

As treatment progressed, I had Parvati simultaneously say her feared statements and ideas and add in the phrase, "I will destroy the planet because I did this exposure therapy and never did enough to help the planet," and, "We will all die in the next century because I did this exposure practice, and it will all be my fault." I also enlisted Parvati's parents to assist with exposure by making random exposure statements within Parvati's hearing, saying phrases such as, "I no longer believe in global warming," or, "I don't think anyone will be able to save the planet. We should make plans to move to Mars now," or, "Parvati just isn't taking global warming seriously. She should really be doing more." I did this to approximate the situation that occurs when a patient gets random intrusive thoughts, so Parvati could improve her ability to ignore the types of things her OCD made her think. Lastly, we found some old incandescent lightbulbs and had Parvati use these in her bedroom.

Once her anxiety was better managed, I had Parvati set realistic goals for addressing her concern about global warming. Her parents agreed to let her use walking and cycling as her method of transportation unless it was unrealistic. Her parents agreed to no longer use plastic shopping bags and they purchased some automatic sensors that turned off lights when no one was in the room. Parvati joined the school's global planet health club and implemented their activities with the rule that she would not allow her OCD to improve on any of the guidelines other club members followed. She also unsubscribed from many blogs and social media sites that had alarmist messages about global warming. She subscribed instead to several news feeds that described good news about success in addressing global warming. She was able to agree to the concept that it was practical and self-compassionate to do some globally corrosive activities, such as using digital devices and plastics, until a better method is developed. She also felt empowered because her family adopted a more ecologically responsible lifestyle due to her influence.

Social justice OCD

Morality-based OCD that comes in the guise of social justice concerns can be difficult to treat because patients often fear the consequence of being publicly humiliated by others for not being properly sensitive, "woke," or aware of the effects of social injustice or of being insensitive to the effects of their own privilege. My clinical experience is that emerging adults who are in university or the later years of high school are more likely to experience obsessions and compulsions about social justice than younger patients. Of particular concern is the fear of "cancel culture," the phenomenon that occurs when others misperceive someone to be unrighteous and use social media to shame the one they find offensive. Many of my patients have feared being "cancelled" even more than being morally incorrect or uncertain. Just as you handle other easier subtypes of OCD that involve risk such as contamination exposures, you also must help your patient reframe the potential consequence of being "cancelled" in order to normalize appropriate risk-taking during ERP and recovery. One of the dilemmas for youth of the 21st century is that improper word choice, no matter how well intended, is assumed to be traumatic for those who are not privileged or who identify with a minority sub-grouping. OCD exaggerates this concern about microaggression and distorts it into trauma of devastating proportions that frightens patients into compulsive word choice, apologizing, rephrasing, editing and moral self-scrutiny. While the phenomenon of microaggression is indeed harmful for minorities, it is also true that overzealous social justice activists can err on the side of refusing to make allowance for misguided good intention during the process of cultural awakening. OCD patients are aware of this social minefield and can exaggerate the consequences of being cancelled for accidentally failing to properly acknowledge their own privilege, failing to feel guilt for their privilege or failing to use the latest most sensitive version of word choice to reflect the values of those who experience discrimination. Therapists can feel intimidated by this situation and err on the side of being too cautious when designing exposure practice or when setting limits for reasonable and healthy behavior with respect to social justice. They might forget that sometimes good intentions are all people have before they begin the process of learning how others who are not like them feel and react. Some cultural bruising and bumping is inevitable and necessary if we are to get close enough to others to be able to understand and better love them better. We need to teach this to our patients to help them become more resilient.

Here is how I address this with patients:

Therapist: "Your OCD has really been torturing you about the possibility of getting cancelled. That must feel terrifying. No one wants to be shunned by others or be so catastrophically misunderstood. Here is the problem. No one can control another person's behavior and your OCD is trying to convince you that you can control what others do if only you are perfect. Do you really believe you could be so perfect no one would find fault with you?"

Patient: "Well, not really when you put it like that."

Therapist: "Good. So, what happens if you really could be perfectly kind and never do anything offensive and someone still takes offense and cancels you? Is that under your control?"

Patient: "Um, no. I guess not. But it would ruin my life."

Therapist: "I agree that it would be unfair, mean and might make life difficult, but whose opinions do you listen to most? The people who deeply understand you and care about you or the people who jump to conclusions and find fault with anyone who disagrees with them?"

Patient: "I would listen to the people who understood me and cared about me, of course."

Therapist: "Well, that is the way most people think. The important thing is to ignore the opinions of people who are not thoughtful or who do not understand your point of view, even when what they say is cruel. Accept that it is impossible to get everyone's approval. What would you have to be like if you could guarantee everyone's approval, even a neo-Nazi or a serial killer's? Wouldn't that mean you would stop being you and must just say what everyone else wanted to hear? How does that sound for being authentic and self-compassionate? Do you want to be that person?"

Patient: "No!"

Therapist: "So, what are you going to listen to? The lie that you cannot live with the accidental disapproval of others or the freedom that comes from accepting that no one can be perfect, including you, and that it is okay when some people fail to see your good intentions and good behaviors?

"We also need to talk about something no one wants to acknowledge. It is the fact that none of us can perfectly avoid microaggressions because we are all raised in different backgrounds that make different incorrect assumptions about others. Part of growing is learning to be humble because you recognize that you are not perfectly able to love others or even yourself. Humility means you forgive yourself for being human, you know what you are good at and what your limitations are, and you do the same for others, even when they hurt you. Do you see the need for that?"

Patient: "So, you are saying that I should not be more sensitive towards the injustices other experience?"

Therapist: "No, I am saying the human mind must learn to stop making assumptions about others and this takes a long time. Every person also has the tendency to put their own mistakes down to the circumstances and to assume that others' mistakes are caused by a bad personality. For example, if I am late to our appointment, I would tell you the traffic was bad, but you would be likely to think I was irresponsible and unprofessional for being late. It means that if others find fault with you and declare you bad, then you forgive them because they are reflecting this mental tendency."

Once your patient can accept the idea that they can never be perfect in their attempts to gain approval for their good intentions, then it is much easier to enter the ERP component of treatment. You will also have to incorporate exposure to the possibility of being cancelled into imaginal exposure, as well as saying and posting statements that may not be perfectly worded to indicate social awareness of inequality and discrimination. You may also have to teach conflict de-escalation skills so the patient can manage classroom or peer discussions about issues of social justice that invite mutual criticism. Patients who feel well prepared to handle the misinformed personal attacks of others will feel more confident about living in the messy moral middle and be less likely to resort to compulsions, reassurance seeking or avoidance.

Patients with social justice concerns also tend to do a lot of reassurance seeking by asking others their opinion of their word choice or actions. They want clarification and reassurance they have not offended others or committed any microaggressions. This could include getting others to review their text messages and social media posts, as well as examining past conversations and interactions. For example, a university student compulsively analyzed how she smiled, spoke and acted when around non-Caucasian students. She repeatedly queried her close friends to ask if her hands, face and words sounded natural and accepting. She would grill them until they gave her reassurance that she was not coming across as prejudiced or as someone who was not familiar and comfortable with other races and ethnicities. Your treatment should be sure to include family or significant others who get trapped into offering reassurance.

Hopefully, you now have some examples and guidelines for being more effective with morality-based scrupulosity OCD. Many of the techniques described for treating scrupulosity will apply to the sub-type addressed in the next chapter: OCD that interacts with LGBTQ+ issues.

If you would like to view a demonstration of how to implement some of the strategies mentioned in this chapter, please go to https://library.jkp.com/redeem using the code ZVEAZDD.

CHAPTER 6

Treating OCD that Interacts with LGBTQ+ Issues

The area of LBTBQ+ issues that affects mental health is nuanced, and complicated by the trauma of stigma, abuse and increased risk for suicide and homicide. I recognize that a single chapter cannot adequately address the multiplicity of concerns of youth who are members of various LGBTQ+ subgroups and who have OCD obsessions that have LGBTQ+ content. Thus, I will do my humble best to describe the ways OCD affects both cisgender straight patients and patients who are exploring their gender identity and sexuality, while acknowledging the ways various LGBTQ+ subcultures might perceive cognitive behavioral interventions. I have been the fortunate beneficiary of LGBTQ+ patients who have bravely corrected my ignorance or misunderstanding of their subcultures. My best advice for you is to continually seek information from members of the LGBTQ+ community to update your understanding of LGBTQ+ culture and help refine the way you understand your patients' expression of OCD. Culture does not cause OCD; however, it can influence the content of OCD. For example, 20 years ago, many of my patients' obsessions centered on being lesbian, gay or bisexual and being rejected or having an unwanted sexual orientation. Now, in the early 21st century, this content is less common. I am more likely to encounter patients whose concern is the uncertainty about not knowing their gender or sexual orientation for sure or feeling shame about being reluctant were they indeed to be LGBTQ+. I still encounter parents who fear the social consequences of their child's gender or sexual orientation or who believe LGBTQ+ identities are against their faith. What is new is parents who are anxiously attempting to affirm their child's LGBTQ+ identity when the patient is not yet able to ascertain their identity or has no LGBTQ+ identity and suffers from OCD that hijacks LGBTQ+ content. Many parents want to avoid the mistake of harming their child's mental health by accidentally indicating rejection of LGBTQ+ identities and are confused as to how OCD might influence their child's behaviors. If the parent is anxiously trying to reassure the child, this can end up confusing the patient further if they misinterpret the parents' reassurances as indication of their identity or feel a need to please the parent by prematurely selecting an identity or sexual orientation. If a parent is as intolerant of uncertainty as OCD patients are, this can be a real risk.

Development of LGBTQ+ identity

It helps to understand how youth develop their identity. Children typically self-identify their gender by their toddler years; however, culture and family attitudes about gender can influence the expression of gender or the willingness to express gender identity. A lack of cultural permission to express variations of cisgender identity may delay the expression of gender that does not conform to physical or chromosomal gender characteristics. Additionally, it is normal for many youths to question their sexual orientation until they begin adolescence and experiment with relationships. Some youth report knowing their entire life they were LGBTQ+ and others report that their awareness of their identity and sexual orientation developed over time and across relationships. Also, there is no known psychological test that confirms a specific LGBTQ+ identity. No therapist or parent can accurately detect a patient's identity because it is something that must be recognized by the patient alone. Additionally, identities can change across the lifespan. For patients with OCD this creates a minefield of uncertainty. Here is how I talk to parents who wish to eliminate uncertainty with respect to the patient's identity:

Therapist: "The problem with trying to gain certainty about your child's identity is that you are accidentally agreeing with your child's OCD that one cannot live with uncertainty. Can you guess how this will interfere with your child's recovery? It will be important for you to learn to live with uncertainty so you can show your child how to do this and help with their exposure practice. What do you think about this idea?"

When parents are anxiously reassuring their child about their LGBTQ+ identity, I enlist the aid of the patient to explain to the parents how this interferes with their OCD. I ask the child to explain what it feels like to see their parent's anxiety about trying to make them feel loved and what it does to their intrusive thoughts and urge to do compulsions or avoidance. This is what this would look like in a session:

Therapist: "I have noticed that you are accidentally trying to get certainty about your child's identity. Unfortunately, only your child can figure out their identity, no matter how much we help them. There is no accurate test of LGBTQ+ identity. It is also normal for many youths to feel uncertain until they have their first romantic relationship or become sexually active. Like most things, they learn through experience rather than thinking their way through it."

Mother: "I just want him to know how much I love him, and I don't want him to ever want to hurt himself."

Therapist: "I can tell you love him very much indeed. It sounds as if you have heard how trans kids are more likely to struggle with mental health concerns. However, I notice that every time Tanner mentions his obsessions about being trans, you get a bit teary-eyed and mention how much you love him, no matter what. I would like to hear what that does to Tanner's OCD when this happens."

Tanner: "Mum, it makes me feel all pitiful and then my OCD starts bothering me more."

Therapist: "How does your OCD bother you more?"

Tanner: "I start wondering if my mum knows something I don't and maybe I really am trans and then I get the thought that I don't want to be trans, and that must mean I hate trans people. Then I start feeling that I have to say being trans is okay and whatever I do next must mean I am trans even though I am not."

Engaging parents who disapprove of LGBTQ+ identities

Some parents will have religious or personal backgrounds that oppose the idea of a child being LGBTQ+. They might wrongly believe that exposure to ideas and images related to LGBTQ+ content might influence a child to become LGBTQ+. This can interfere with engagement in treatment when ERP needs to include content about being LGBTQ+, or content the patient considers related to sexuality. This poses a delicate situation for the therapist because it is the therapist's job to promote successful treatment while respecting family culture. It is also the therapist's job to accurately represent the best scientific knowledge about mental health and mental wellness for the benefit of the patient and their family. I have several guidelines for handling parental concerns while respecting their concerns.

First, I explain that no one can accurately predict or control the developing nature of a child's gender identity or sexual orientation. It is not something one can cause or prevent. It just happens. I explain the real mental health risk for parents who disapprove of or reject their child's identity along with the negative multiplicative effect it will have on their child's struggle to overcome OCD. I also explain that science has shown that exposure to oppositive gender behaviors does not cause LGBTQ+ identities. I remind them that no one gets to control or predict exactly who their child will become in any area, not just LGBTQ+. I tell them that the risk for suicide, depression, anxiety and substance abuse increases the more a child perceives rejection from their environment, and I challenge them to keep the doors open for family unity that allows for unexpected differences. I also remind them that medical and mental health professionals do not consider LGBTQ+ to be a mental health diagnosis; rather, the mental health problems of being LGBTQ+ are the direct result of the stigma and abuse LGBTQ+ people experience.

Second, I ask them if they could for the time being suspend their judgment for the sake of OCD recovery and refrain from making any comments about their point of view to their child so long as we are working together. I ask them if they have ever had something they wish they could change about themselves but been unsuccessful in changing, such as being overweight, disorganized, a smoker or quick to anger. Once I identify something that cannot be readily changed, I ask the parents how it feels when others tell them they should change, when others disapprove of them or give them nasty glances because they are that way. I ask whether these glances, advice or criticisms motivate them to change, or make them feel shame and rejection. I explain that their comments or facial expressions have the same effect on their child. I also have them write down a list of helpful reframes to their critical thoughts to review and use this to avoid unhelpful behaviors during treatment. Here is an example:

- I do not want to unnecessarily make my child feel judged or rejected when they most need my support to recover from OCD.

- Ever since there have been families, there have been children who disappoint their parents because children are their own separate beings. I can learn to live with this like others have done before me.

- My child will recover from their OCD faster if I keep my opinions to myself about LGBTQ+.

- Just because I disapprove of something does not mean I have to talk to my child about it.

- The immediate big danger is my child's mental health being destroyed by OCD. I want them to focus on recovery instead of my opinions about LGBTQ+.

Exposure with sexual content for youth

Many therapists and parents wonder where to draw the boundary for the type of sexual content that might be necessary for successful imaginal or in vivo exposure practice. Many therapists make the mistake of assuming that inappropriate content, such as pornography, should be used for imaginal or in vivo exposure, but this is not necessary. If you recognize that children at various ages have different perceptions of things related to sexual activity and gender, then you will realize it is possible to avoid the misstep of having to resort to using pornographic websites. Professional ethics dictates that therapists do not expose children or teens to disturbing or developmentally inappropriate sexual content unless the patient's OCD has already done so. Instead, I determine what the content of the child's OCD is, and their developmental understanding of that content, and use this as my guide for designing exposure. For example, a six-year-old might obsess about kissing same-gender peers, but the kiss they picture is akin to a peck on the cheek. A 13-year-old might have the same obsession and experience intrusive thoughts about deep prolonged kisses and groping a same-gender peer's genitals or breasts. A 17-year-old with the same obsession might have intrusive thoughts that resemble a script for an adult film.

An additional concern for therapists who work with children is to avoid the accidental appearance of being a sexual predator, especially if the therapist is male. Government and police agencies flag internet traffic on sites that portray sexual images and stories about pedophilic contacts with minors. Police detectives know that anyone who works with children is at higher risk for being a pediatric sexual predator, and you might unwittingly become a target should your computer be detected conducting inappropriate pedophilic internet searches. The best way I can suggest for avoiding this dilemma is to never use your digital devices for any searches that involve pedophilic content. Should you have a patient who is in late adolescence or an emerging adult, you can usually achieve good exposure by using imaginal exposure that the patient creates. You can instruct the patient to imagine doing the things their OCD fears without having to depict actual sex acts and while having the patient describe their anxious reaction. You can also use images that are safe but provoke anxiety, such as looking at children wearing bathing costumes, underwear, pajamas or gymnastics leotards. Unlike working with adult patients, in which one can be more explicit or might use more graphic images, you can let the patient stay in the zone their OCD imagination has created without accidentally and inappropriately expanding their library of sexual imagery.

Some patients, especially teens and emerging adults, may be engaging in reassurance seeking and checking compulsions that involve surfing on pornographic websites to verify how they respond to various images. They may attempt to masturbate to images or stories to "make sure" they have a particular sexual orientation. They might gaze at nude images to examine how they feel about male or female appearance. Normally this would not pose a problem unless the patient has reached the age of majority and is clearly surfing content about minors. You may need to warn your patient about the danger of searching for youthful images after reaching adulthood.

You also need to discriminate between a patient's doubt versus dislike of LGBTQ+ obsessions. Patients with doubting intrusive thoughts will need to do exposure to uncertainty. For example, they will need to repeat phrases that express uncertainty and enter situations that provoke uncertainty until they get comfortable with these thoughts and situations. Patients who dislike and fear LGBTQ+ thoughts will need to do exposure to desiring and inviting those thoughts. For example, they may need to repeat phrases such as "Secretly and subconsciously I want to be queer," do things they imagine represent being queer or make public statements about being okay if they were to discover they were queer. Some patients may experience both types of reactions to intrusive thoughts and will need to do both types of ERP.

Here is a chart to help you fashion exposure for various obsessions typical in LGBTQ+-focused OCD:

Obsession and compulsion	Exposure with response prevention
Afraid to notice same gender peers in the locker room and keeps eyes down for fear it means she is a lesbian	Repeat "I must be lesbian," count how many blonde-haired girls are in gym class, count how many girls are wearing necklaces

cont.

Obsession and compulsion	Exposure with response prevention
Notices genital sensations when with peers to determine if they have a sexual response that will inform them if they are gay, straight or bisexual	Repeat, "I will never know what I prefer," say to self when looking at everyone, "This one is going to be the love of my life," drink caffeinated beverages to feel more "aroused" when looking at peers and say to self, "I am really getting a reaction to this one"
Trans girl won't touch anything that touches her penis, refuses to look at penis, avoids looking at male torso area	Do exposure to brief glances at others and own torso area in mirror, increase length of gaze and say aloud, "I guess I am not really a girl," do brief touches on the outside of own underwear, inside underwear and eventually own penis, look at males and list type of jeans fly, zipper or button, look at male swimsuit and underwear ads
Compulsively changes identity every few days after getting intrusive thoughts about being wrong about their gender identity	Tell others they do not yet know their gender identity, use they/them pronouns, keep the "they/them" identity until no longer anxious about uncertainty, repeat aloud, "I will never be clear about who I am and never be able to have a good future because I won't know"
Repeatedly tries to clear mind of intrusive thoughts about being gay because he does not want to be gay and is ashamed that this means he is not accepting of gay people. Avoids known LGBTQ+ peers for fear of insulting them	Look at underwear and bathing costume ads while saying aloud, "This must mean I am gay and there is nothing I can do to change it," repeatedly say, "I must hate gay people because I do not want to be one," imagine meeting gays and blurting out, "I hate gay people!", start conversations and text chats with known LGBTQ+ peers
Avoids all situations and conversations that mention LGBTQ+ issues to avoid intrusive thoughts about not knowing gender identity or sexual orientation for certain	Read media that mention celebrities known to be LGBTQ+, surf LGBTQ+ websites and media, ask others their opinion about LGBTQ+ issues, repeat the phrase, "I will never figure out who I am. I will be the only one in my school or university who doesn't know who they are. I won't be able to marry because I will never know who I am"

Addressing uncertainty

I just described possible exposure practice for uncertainty about identity. You also need to discuss with patients the role reassurance seeking plays in cementing their intolerance of uncertainty. One advantage of current culture surrounding the LGBTQ+ community is the acknowledgement that people change throughout their lifespan, and it is not necessary to have a single permanent sense of self. It is helpful for patients to learn that uncertainty about anything is normal for all human beings. The enemy is OCD, not the uncertainty. Having the patient read real-life coming-out stories about how others experienced uncertainty or change in their gender identity or sexual orientation can be appropriately validating of their experience of uncertainty. Sharing your own stories of being initially repelled by the idea of dating or sex until you experienced your first crush or relationship can be very helpful. For patients whose initial sexual experiences were disappointing, you can share how common this experience is for people because sexual behaviors are learned, require an element of practice and acquired comfort with one's sexuality, and lack of fear about unintended pregnancy or disease transmission. You may need to obtain the parent's permission to discuss these issues should they believe it inappropriate to discuss such matters prior to marriage.

When both OCD and LGBTQ+ identity collide

The two strands of burgeoning self-awareness about gender identity or sexual orientation that is LGBTQ+, and OCD about the same issues, can be complicated to tease apart and treat. Some therapists who specialize in helping children and teens transition or affirm their sexual orientation may consider it offensive to use imaginal exposure that appears to deny the possibility of an emerging LGBTQ+ identity, or consider it traumatic to force exposure to images of gender or sexual expression that might trigger feelings of anxiety, distaste or lack of acceptance. These concerns are valid because many LGBTQ+ children and teens may have acquired shaming or traumatic ideas about being LGBTQ+. On the other hand, untreated or poorly treated OCD tends to be chronic and potentially disabling. I would not want to add to the already heavy burden a patient might experience on top of being LGBTQ+. When this situation occurs, I attempt to clarify the symptoms that are clearly OCD and their negative effect on the patient. Then I work hard to get the patient's support system to understand

and accept the need for OCD treatment alongside the need for affirmation and acceptance of the patient's developing identity and sexual orientation. I want to avoid the patient and parents getting confused by competing messages from the LGBTQ+ community and the community of OCD therapists. To that end, I prefer to confer with anyone who appears to consider proposed ERP as traumatizing or contradictory, to enlist their aid and help them understand my full support of the patient's status as LGBTQ+. I also help the patient to clarify the difference between intrusive OCD thoughts and other thoughts. I do it like this:

Therapist: "Your OCD looks as if it makes it really confusing to be you. I may not be an expert on LGBTQ+ issues, but I do know that if we do not help you overcome your OCD, you will be miserable, and I want to prevent that. Let's look at how to tell the difference between an OCD thought and other thoughts that might be useful or important to notice. This is the same way that OCD experts can tell if someone has OCD no matter what their OCD gets stuck on. This way we can both feel confident about which thoughts need exposure practice. Would you like to learn the formula?"

Patient: "Yes."

Therapist: "I will draw this on the whiteboard and then you can compare your thoughts to the formula to see for yourself if a thought is from OCD and know the best way to treat it."

Then I'll draw a chart that looks like the one below and have the patient compare various intrusive thoughts and other distressing thoughts about LGBTQ+ issues to categorize them.

Here is an example of how I might categorize the patient's thoughts:

OCD thoughts	Non-OCD thoughts
• Make me anxious or scared • Make me feel doubt or more confused • Make me want to do something to get rid of them, avoid them or feel better about them • Don't really make sense when I am not so anxious • Don't make sense to others who know me • Do not lead to anything that makes me feel clearer about who I am or what I want to do • Confuse my ability to make decisions	• Help me better understand myself • Make sense to me and others who know me • Make it easier to make decisions • Can upset me, but still make it easier to understand myself or others • Can sit comfortably in my mind without having to do something right away to get rid of them or figure out what they mean

My hope is that you now have more confidence and clarity on how to design and implement treatment for your patients who experience LGBTQ+-focused OCD. The next chapter will help you treat patients whose obsessions focus on the nature of their existence or their ability to discern the presence of their existence.

If you would like to view a demonstration of how to implement some of the strategies mentioned in this chapter, please go to https://library.jkp.com/redeem using the code ZVEAZDD.

CHAPTER 7

Treating Existential OCD

Obsessions and Compulsions about the Nature of Existence and the Afterlife

The category of existential OCD can sometimes be misdiagnosed as psychosis or delusions. I have had more than a few patients referred to me with the warning they were on the edge of a psychotic break or showing early signs of psychosis or delusions. Why? Because the obsessions and compulsions that accompany existential OCD can be bizarre. When bizarre is accompanied by intolerance of uncertainty, then patients can appear to resemble psychotic or delusional patients.

CASE EXAMPLE

Liza was a 15-year-old who read lots of science fiction about multiple planes of existence and dead people being brought back to life to become cyborg beings. After reading about people who believed there were multiple planes of existence as part of their spirituality, she began getting intrusive thoughts, "What if I am not in the plane of existence I am supposed to be? What if I am not really alive? What if I am a cyborg and this is not my original form of existence?" She began making up compulsive tests to verify her existence by pinching herself, counting to one hundred while making sure there were no shimmers in her peripheral vision that might indicate an alternative existential plane, or asking family and close friends if she seemed like herself. She began researching quantum physics to seek reassurance about her existence, but this just increased her anxiety. She began fearing going to sleep after getting the intrusive thought, "What if it is not sleep but I am being put to sleep to be transported to another plane of existence?" She also began feeling depersonalized and this made her suicidal because she obsessed that these sensations proved she was not truly alive and present in the proper existential plane.

Examples of existential OCD obsessions

Patients with existential OCD have obsessions centered on verifying their existence, the quality of their existence or the quality or reality of their existence after death. Their OCD attempts to eliminate the uncertainty of the nature of their existence, their consciousness or the presence of consciousness and quality of life after death. Obsessions and intrusive thoughts may be triggered by science fiction media, or peer discussions about the nature of existence and death. Sometimes, religious education might trigger obsessions as the patient ponders what it might be like to be aware after one's death. Inevitably, the intrusive thoughts are unpleasant and frightening, such as being aware that one is dead and trapped in a coffin underground for all eternity, being on a separate plane of existence from one's family or friends or being lost in an alternative universe. Obsessions can also be focused on proving the fact of one's existence without being able to come to the obvious conclusion from Descartes' philosophical "I think therefore I am." Here are examples of existential obsessions and compulsions to help you better detect their presence and not mistake them for psychotic or delusional phenomena:

Obsession	Compulsion
What if I am not really here?	Asking others how they know the patient, when they met them and what the shared history is, pinching self and trying to recall all their life memories
What if I am caught up in a matrix of alternative realities and I am not in the right one?	Looking for subtle changes in the appearance or vocal tone of others, looking in the periphery for evidence of shimmers or shadow beings, asking parents and friends if the movie, The Matrix is real

What if I am alive, inside my decaying body in a coffin and no one will know it?	Checking pulse and breathing to make sure they are alive, asking parents when they will die, asking about what life after death is like, counting down time passed to keep track of time left to live, reading about life after death and reading about people who were declared dead and returned to life
What if I never am truly connected to myself in my body? What if an alien has abducted me and this is why I feel weird?	Repeated scrutiny of their body for signs of dissociation, depersonalization, derealization, asking questions about how others feel, if they ever feel like them, reading about people who have out-of-body experiences or who were abducted by aliens
What if I do something dangerous because I do not know who I am? What if I have a hidden dangerous personality?	Hypervigilance for feeling weird, reading about the meaning of existence, compulsive praying to know their real self, asking others how they know they are and who they think they are, getting into discussions about the nature of existence and what makes good people different from bad people
What if I am not real? What if this is just my imagination?	Questioning others about how to know if they are real, reading about what reality is, compulsive journaling about awareness of self, asking others how they know they are real

Depersonalization/derealization and existential OCD

This particular subtype can also interact with internal sensations of anxiety, such as depersonalization, derealization and feeling lightheaded. Patients misinterpret these internal sensations that are the product of anxiety as possible evidence of being in an altered state of existence. For example, in the case of Liza, above, she mistook the symptom of depersonalization that can occur with a panic attack or severe anxiety as proof that she was not fully connected to her current life. It is likely that her spiraling anxiety brought on her symptoms of depersonalization; however, she did not know that depersonalization could occur as part of an anxiety disorder. Many patients and therapists are familiar with the cardiac and gastrointestinal symptoms of anxiety, but are unaware that feeling surreal, dissociated, depersonalized or lightheaded are also symptoms of severe anxiety. Additionally, some therapists subscribe to the lore that depersonalization must be a severe and treatment refractory condition because they associate it only with depersonalization/derealization disorder. The criteria for this disorder require that a patient have a consistent feeling of depersonalization or derealization while being able to correctly stay in touch with reality during these episodes. These symptoms cannot be caused by substances or medications and the patient must feel distressed about feeling depersonalized or derealized. Lastly and most importantly, these symptoms cannot be caused by other disorders, such as OCD or other disorders.

Patients who have OCD that includes the experience of depersonalization or derealization will be caught up in compulsions, avoidance and reassurance seeking, unlike the symptoms of depersonalization/derealization disorder. It will also be clear that their depersonalization and derealization occur in the context of anxiety about their intrusive thoughts or after they experience surges in anxiety due to the failure of compulsions and avoidance to achieve quick relief. I help patients who mistake these physical sensations by using interoceptive exposure practice and explaining the physiology of anxiety attacks. Interoceptive exposure is exposure practice that produces the internal sensations feared by the patient that often accompany anxiety and panic attacks. It seeks to induce feared physical sensations so the patient discovers they can manage the sensations by calm acceptance and can even increase or decrease them depending on their posture, breathing pattern or hypervigilance. My goal is to teach patients that their physical sensations are harmless, though uncomfortable, and survivable, and can even be influenced by their behavior and attitude about these sensations. This treatment is the same as that I would use with patients who experience panic disorder. Here is how I worked with Liza using interoceptive exposure:

Therapist: "Liza, it seems that you and your OCD have misunderstood what happens when you feel depersonalized, as if you are not inside your body, or derealized, as if you are not really part of the present moment and are disconnected from reality. That can be really frightening when you do not understand what is happening or why it happens. Would you like to hear what science knows about what makes people feel Like this?

Liza: "What do you mean?"

Therapist: "We know when people get anxious, they tense their shoulders, hunch forward and get into a protective fear posture. (I illustrate this posture.) All people and animals do this when they feel fear or sense danger. They also start breathing more shallowly and rapidly. This makes them exhale too much carbon dioxide. Carbon dioxide is what your body produces after it uses the oxygen from the air. When you exhale too much carbon dioxide, you make your body feel odd. The odd feelings are what everyone notices when they have anxiety or a panic attack. Some people feel some of the odd feelings and others feel different odd feelings. The odd feelings can be rapid heartbeats, sweating, cold chills, hot flushes, dizziness, feelling as if you cannot get enough air, feeing a sense of impending doom, depersonalization, derealization, butterflies in the tummy, or feeling that your heart is pounding out of your chest. Do you recognize any of these sensations when your OCD gets triggered?"

Liza: "Yes, I feel my heartbeats and that I am losing my mind, too."

Therapist: "That is a good observation. Those are symptoms of anxiety, just like feeling fast heartbeats or shakiness. What I think happens when your OCD gets triggered is that your body gets anxious and then your OCD misinterprets the anxiety symptoms of depersonalization and derealization as evidence of something being wrong with your reality. Would you like to do an experiment to see how you can increase and decrease this sensation just by changing your breathing?"

Liza: "I guess so. What is involved?"

Distinguishing between existential OCD and psychosis

I have occasionally been referred a patient with existential OCD who has been misdiagnosed as being psychotic. This happened because other mental health professionals mistook the bizarre content of the patient's obsessions for delusions. For example, what would you do if a patient told you, "I am afraid I am living in another dimension that seems like this one, but it's a copy of the real one, only slightly different," or, "I am afraid I am not truly alive. What if I am dead and this is all not real?" or, "I am afraid I am caught in a wormhole. How do I know for sure that I am where I am supposed to be in the timeline of life?" These statements certainly sound bizarre and nonsensical, but OCD can take any idea and create doubt that causes anxiety. The distinguishing characteristic of OCD is how it plays on doubt and leads to compulsive attempts to alleviate anxiety. The distinguishing characteristics of psychosis include significant disruptions in thinking, speech, motor behavior, daily functioning and the presence of delusions and hallucinations. When OCD occurs, the patient recognizes that their thoughts are bizarre and unwanted, but when psychosis occurs, the patient believes in the delusion (McClellan, 2018).

OCD can take any idea and create doubt that causes anxiety.

Psychotic patients may react to their delusions, but not to get rid of them—as is typical of OCD—because they are unable to distinguish between reality and delusion or hallucination. Their thinking, speech and behavior patterns are otherwise normal. Acute psychotic states come on quickly with no apparent warning, with a lack of a clear trigger, as seen in OCD. Often acute psychotic reactions in youth are the result of severe stress or a reaction to medication. Schizophrenia tends to follow a developmental pattern of slow onset of unusual behavior and thinking in the teen years until the latter teens or early twenties when delusions, hallucinations and unusual behaviors manifest. Lastly, there is hereditary risk for both anxiety disorders and psychotic disorders that tends to run in families. If there is no apparent family history of psychotic disorders, then it is more unlikely a patient might develop the same. Likewise, when there is a family history of anxiety disorders, it is much more likely that the patient has OCD, no matter how unusual the content of their obsessions. The prevalence rate for OCD in youth is 1–3 percent, whereas the prevalence rate for schizophrenia in youth is only 0.23 percent, making the diagnosis of OCD much more likely (James, Farrell & Zimmer-Gembeck, 2017).

Using interoceptive exposure

Interoceptive exposure, as mentioned earlier in this chapter, means deliberately creating the feared physical sensations of anxiety that accompany a patient's trigger situations, whether it be thoughts, images or other experiences. Toward this end, I have patients do things that mimic or induce the sensations of intense anxiety. This can make exposure practice more powerful because it mimics what happens when the patient has a spontaneous panic attack (four or more sudden symptoms of anxiety) or a limited symptom attack (three or fewer sudden symptoms of anxiety). Thus, patients learn to manage both their emotional, cognitive and physical response to an anxiety trigger. Toward this end, I use techniques, which I will list in a table below, to induce the dreaded feelings of depersonalization, derealization or other symptoms the patient misinterprets as loss of self or loss of reality. Doing this practice serves two purposes: showing the patient the factual origin of their symptoms as an expression of behavioral changes in breathing that accompany anxiety, and showing the patient that they can handle even the most feared cluster of symptoms. It helps to overcome the phenomenon that many patients experience when they feel some degree of safety doing exposure in the presence of the therapist by recreating a more realistic and frightening experience of anxiety. Here is a list of exercises that will induce the physical sensations typical of a limited symptom or panic attack:

Interoceptive exposure	Sensations targeted
Acute hyperventilation Step 1: Huffing full breaths in and out rapidly, as though you are sprinting at top speed, until you feel weird Step 2: Continuing to acutely hyperventilate after reaching the point of feeling weird to intensify the sensation and attempt to deliberately induce a panic attack	Dizzy, lightheaded, hot flushes, cold chills, depersonalization, derealization, butterflies in tummy, tunnel vision, sense of loss of control, rapid heartbeats, tingling in extremities or face, sense of impending doom, air hunger, tightness in chest, dry mouth
Spinning in a desk chair, or spinning while standing and being spotted by a therapist	Dizzy, lightheaded, unsteady

cont.

Interoceptive exposure	Sensations targeted
Sitting while placing head between knees for two minutes and then quickly raising head to sitting position	Dizzy, feeling unreal, lightheaded

When I use interoceptive practice, I use it specifically to address the fear of feeling depersonalized or derealized. The patient learns to create the symptoms they fear and test their anxious hypothesis that these feelings are an indication of being out of touch with reality or not being fully present in their current existence. Once they can tolerate interoceptive exposure and no longer dread the sensation, I combine interoceptive exposure with imaginal exposure. This can be very effective. I do this by first inducing the feared physical sensations and then adding in feared statements, feared feedback (me saying that I no longer believe they have OCD, but instead really are subject to switches in reality) and feared scripts about becoming all the things they fear. I then use their feared sensations as "evidence" of their fears being real. I continue this form of combined exposure until the patient no longer startles, refrains from asking for reassurance and shows they can handle it by laughing, relaxing or saying, "I get it." This is how I might do this type of exposure:

Therapist: "You have done a great job getting used to the feeling of being dissociated. Let's see if we can make this practice work even better for you by increasing the challenge. Let's hyperventilate for one minute after you start feeling weird. Just raise your finger when you first notice feeling weird. Then I will tell you to stop and I will begin saying things to you to see if we can scare your OCD. Your job is to agree out loud with anything I say? Do you think you can do that?"

Patient: "Yes."

Therapist: "Okay, let's go!"

Patient raises their finger.

Therapist: "That is fantastic! You are really doing a great job pushing back against your OCD. I am so impressed by your courage. Keep making it feel worse until you feel as out of your body as possible. Okay, now stop. Now, I am going to see if I can scare your OCD. Are you ready?"

Patient: "I'm not sure."

Therapist: "Then that means you are going to get even more value out of this exposure practice. Here we go. You know, as I watch you there, you do not seem to be all the way there. It's as if there is a shimmer or something and it makes me wonder if you are really here or if this is a figment of my imagination or even if we are on two different planes of reality. I am feeling really confused. I normally feel totally connected to all my patients and you have a different feel from other kids. What do you think?"

Patient: "You are right, and you are scaring me!"

Therapist: "Fantastic! This is the sign that this is some really powerful exposure that can kick some OCD. I am so proud of you. I am starting to feel that we are not connected like two human beings should be connected. You keep fading in and out. What if you are not really here with me? Now, agree with me out loud."

Patient: "We are not really in this room together. What if we are in different realities and I am the only one in my reality?"

Therapist: "I am not even sure you have OCD. I think I have been wrong in your case. You must be my first case of alternative realities. I am so sorry, but I am professionally obligated to tell you that you do not have OCD, and something really is out of sync with your reality and presence. Perhaps you should consult an astral physicist?"

Exposure with response prevention to trigger situations is also important. Many patients with existential OCD fear hearing information that might make them think about their obsessions, might trigger intrusive thoughts or might be fictional depictions of feared situations. You will need to identify all the behaviors that interfere with recovery, including mental checking, reassurance-seeking activities and questions, including those that seem innocent and directed toward scientific inquiry, such as, "What do you think of the different viewpoints of various philosophers or scientists on how there are many different realities and how time can bend in on itself?" or, "How do you know you are real?" or, "How do you know what happens after we die?" Teens and emerging adults can get caught in reassurance seeking conversations about esoteric scientific theories of time, wormholes or other phenomena that are very difficult to comprehend, let alone imagine, and trap well-intentioned adults into compulsive conversations. Youth who enjoy this type of discourse can reach a conclusion while allowing for uncertainty or to just enjoy the idea of things beyond our current awareness or imagination. Patients with OCD will get increasingly anxious and circular in their thinking when they enter these conversations. Healthy discussion about the nature of existence will feel interesting, creative and productive, unless OCD is at play. The goal of treatment is to increase tolerance for the uncertainty about the nature of existence so the patient can learn to contemplate normal and curious self-reflection. Here is a sample of typical compulsions seen in this population:

Compulsions
Reading science fiction to gain certainty about OCD triggers, reading theoretical physics, philosophy, mystical religious literature, or blogs speculating on the nature of existence
Avoiding any media that suggest alternative realities or depictions of the afterlife
Having repeated conversations to get reassurance about the nature of existence, the afterlife or the awareness of others or self
Repeatedly checking oneself for awareness of self, being present or feeling fully present and conscious
Asking others if they recognize the patient or the situation or have shared history with the patient they both remember, inquiring about life after death experiences and media to gain reassurance

Response prevention

Many patients with existential OCD must spend extra time focusing on response prevention because they have mental checking and mental recall rituals. These rituals can be rapid and ubiquitous. It is relatively easy to ban significant others from providing reassurance and to put a ban on compulsive media use, or to do exposure to feared media triggers without avoidance. Getting a patient to discontinue mental rituals can be tricky and painstaking.

Healthy conversation about the nature of existence and death

Let's assume you have successfully used the previously mentioned techniques to decrease your patient's anxiety, increase their tolerance of uncertainty and reduce their compulsions and avoidance. How do you discuss the legitimate questions their OCD has mutilated? Just as it is the goal in treating religious scrupulosity OCD to help the patient learn a healthy way to participate in their faith community, it is also wise to teach patients how to do the same with the big questions about the nature of existence and death. You need to help the patient and their family understand that the problem is not with asking or thinking about these questions, but rather the willingness to accept uncertainty about ineffable things we can only accept but not necessarily prove. For example, I might explain to a patient that we all know there is air, but we cannot see it or feel it unless it is moving. We might be able to measure windspeed, but we could still have uncertainty because we cannot see air, unless we use scientific instruments to detect molecules of the components of air. The same is true for knowing someone is a person or knowing one is present in a situation. We can see the effect of the person on what they say and do, and we see how people are different from each other in the way they use words and behave, but how do we measure and prove the existence of a specific person unless they do something? We assume that people are here because they think and act, just like air responds to different atmospheric pressures that create wind. Likewise, we assume someone is dead because they can no longer think, act or function and begin decaying, but we do not have a way to prove what happened to a person's essence, or soul. If we believe in our existence or an afterlife, then we must assume our existence despite having no easy way to prove what exactly happened when we became alive or what will happen when we die.

I explain to patients the reason philosophers and scientists have been asking the same questions for thousands of years is because humans like to wonder about what it means to be a human. This is something unique about humans. OCD likes to take advantage of the uncertainty and turn it into something painful by convincing patients they must be the first person to get the answer right, even though no one else has been able to achieve this. It is not fair to have to prove things no one else can prove.

I also explain that OCD has a tricky way of making people think about their thinking that is unlike people who do not have OCD. In their case, OCD has got stuck on making them think about their awareness of being human and accidentally made them doubt who they are, where they are and what might happen. They no longer must believe the worst-case scenario thoughts that OCD also suggests. They can choose to believe the kinds of thoughts people without OCD experience, such as, "Since I am aware of me, that must mean I am real," or, "I don't have to understand it all. No one does. I can learn to accept what other people do. Just because I get a scary thought does not make it real," or, "Since this is an OCD thought, it is a big fat lie!" I tell patients that most people do not think about their thinking because they know it's more fun to think about other things and they deliberately ignore intrusive thoughts, even when they are scary. They instinctively recognize their thoughts are weird and therefore a waste of time. I ask the patient to label their thoughts as "annoying distractions" or "OCD blather." Then, I practice saying aloud the patient's intrusive thoughts while they reply, "This is just an annoying thought," or, "This is just OCD blather." This is a form of positive practice that helps the patient learn a healthy response to an intrusive thought.

Some patients may need a ban on reading or watching esoteric media about the nature of existence for a time following treatment. They may need an extended period to avoid triggering situations so they can consolidate their ability to notice and ignore intrusive existential thoughts and not be sucked into unnecessary speculation that feeds OCD. I maintain a ban on existential media until the patient can readily manage spontaneous intrusive thoughts and triggers without resuming compulsions. Once they can do this, they are ready to take on more difficult challenges outside the therapy session, such as reading provoking materials or watching provoking movies.

Interrupting mental rituals

The easiest way to interrupt mental rituals is to find ways for the patient to distract themselves with other activities until the urge to examine their thinking or feelings passes. Patients who are constantly engaged in mental rituals may need to start with very small goals of simply learning to switch their attention from their anxiety to something else before they can learn to pay close attention to other thoughts. When I have patients who tell me they always give in to the urge to do mental checking, mental analysis or mental scanning, I first work on breaking this automatic cycle of OCD. Once the patient learns these skills, they often realize they have the capacity to say "No" to their compulsive urges and are more willing to attempt other more effortful activities that might take up their attention. My experience has been that many well-intentioned therapists prematurely attempt to teach meditation skills or non-judgmental self-observation skills before the patient has the belief or ability to notice things besides OCD. Patients first need the ability to pay attention to non-OCD thoughts. I have a suggestion for training the ability to selectively turn away from non-OCD thoughts.

First, use present moment awareness practice in very small increments over many practice trials. I do this by telling the patient to notice their OCD urge and then tell me something they observe that takes effort to notice, such as the colors in my carpet, a sound outside my office, the sensation of the waistband of their clothing or one thing they smell. Success is being able to do the task. I do this 30–50 times, or as many times as necessary until the patient says it more readily. Each time, after they correctly report an observation, I say, "Fantastic! You just broke away from your OCD. You are in control of what you pay attention to." I assign home practice with the parent or in response to a recording we make of the session and tell them their goal is simply to follow directions. Success means being able to do the task rapidly and without great effort. It is okay if OCD interrupts the process early in practice. As practice progresses, the patient should experience fewer interruptions.

Next, I ask the patient to notice their OCD thoughts and compulsive urges and instruct them to do a more difficult task, such as identifying five things in my office that are five different colors, or five different sounds they hear outside my room or five body sensations they feel in five different parts of their body. I continue to give the same feedback as above. When the patient can readily do this and not get interrupted each time by OCD, I advance the task and begin asking them to do other more difficult tasks, such as counting backwards from two hundred by sevens, telling me the names of every pet their family has ever had, the names and birthdays of everyone in their family, five places they would like to visit and why. I try to pick either high interest, non-OCD-related topics or things that take some degree of concentration. Once the patient succeeds at these tasks, I have them use a handheld digital game device, read a paragraph from a book from my shelf, fill out a crossword, complete a wordsearch puzzle or do a sheet of math problems rapidly. My goal is to gradually mimic the types of things a patient might naturally do with their time or mind when at home or school.

Once the patient can do the previously mentioned tasks that take five to seven minutes without getting distracted by OCD, I assign a series of these tasks for scheduled practice at home, regardless of whether the OCD is bothering them at that time. Again, success is being able to complete the task, even if OCD interrupts. I avoid asking them to do the tasks in response to OCD at this stage, because I want the patient to discover they can selectively focus on pleasant or neutral activities even if OCD interrupts. Once the patient can do these three separate times in a day for several days at a time, I begin to ask them to use this distraction technique when OCD tries to derail their mind into mental rituals. This may mean loading digital devices with special high-interest games that can only be played for "OCD" practice and not at other times, to preserve their appeal. This same technique can be used for body-focused obsessions and compulsions, such as compulsive monitoring of breathing and swallowing. Some patients can advance rapidly through this protocol and others may take several months to achieve the ability to turn away from their mental rituals.

Magical thinking

Some patients may fear their intrusive thoughts about existence or death, as they believe simply thinking about them will make them come true. Exposure for these patients should focus on gradually getting the patient to wish, hope and pray that their worse fear comes true. Thought-action fusion is a prominent feature for these patients and exposure practice needs to challenge the idea that thinking about something makes it more likely to happen. Here are suggestions of various exposure ideas you can use to help these patients:

Exposure practice	Response prevention
Say aloud, "What if someone is not really here?" Therapist makes the same statement about themselves	No reassurance seeking or checking
Say aloud, "What if I am not really here?" Therapist makes the same statement about themselves	No reassurance seeking or checking
Say aloud, "I hope I am not really here and this is all an illusion." Therapist makes the same statement about themselves	No reassurance seeking or checking
Say aloud, "I know I am not real and I will never know if I really exist." Therapist says, "I am not sure I recognize you. Who are you?"	No reassurance seeking or checking
Say aloud, "When I blink my eyes, I will wake up in a new dimension even though it looks the same." Therapist says, "Is there someone else in here? Did I hear or see something or someone?" Therapist leaves the room to look for the patient	No reassurance seeking or checking. No correcting the therapist when they "look" for the patient

Lastly, you can have the patient put up signs and post-it notes in their home, bedroom and on their belongings that say, "How do you know you are really here? Is this real? Who are you really? What if you are the only one who is here? What if this is all an illusion?" You can make similar signs for other existential fears that are analogous, such as, "What if you are dead? What if you are the only one alive? What if death is like life, just trapped in a coffin?" The idea is to deliberately trigger the patient's obsessions to give them the opportunity to practice labeling the thoughts as just being OCD and therefore worth ignoring, and then re-directing their attention to something useful, pleasant or productive.

I hope you now understand how to better assess and treat existential OCD. Next, I will talk about what happens when OCD invades romance and romantic relationships.

If you would like to view a demonstration of how to implement some of the strategies mentioned in this chapter, please go to https://library.jkp.com/redeem using the code ZVEAZDD.

CHAPTER 8

Treating Relationship OCD

Perfect Love, Obsessions and Compulsions

Relationship OCD, or ROCD, occurs when patients get obsessions about the quality of their romantic relationships, the quality of their attraction to a partner, the suitability of their partner or the significance of their partner's flaws. Small, typically insignificant flaws can grow into disproportionate seemingly catastrophic issues. Patients can obsess about whether they love someone enough, whether they are in love, whether they have sufficient sexual attraction to a partner, whether they should break up because they dislike a mole on their partner's shoulder, whether their partner properly expresses love to the patient, and more. Although the issues reflected in OCD concerns may be common to many, the defining characteristic is the intrusiveness of thoughts, the need for reassurance and checking, the anxiety the intrusive thoughts create and the patient's desperate need for a quick resolution for the obsession. Here are a few examples that illustrate ROCD.

CASE EXAMPLES

Cassie, a 17-year-old, was involved with her first serious relationship in which she had told her partner she loved her and vice versa. Shortly after her first declaration of love, she began obsessing about whether her love was true, following an argument with her partner. Her intrusive thoughts were, "What if we are not meant for each other? Our love is doomed. I wouldn't have got so mad if I truly loved her." She began examining her feelings for her partner and would hesitate each time she said something affectionate to make sure it was "true," only to become more confused about what she really felt. She had thought about breaking up only to feel bereft about the idea of loss of the relationship. She also began compulsively making up "tests" to see if her love was true, by randomly selecting unrelated events to see if they happened and therefore indicated a positive answer. For example, "If she texts me in the next 15 minutes, then it means our love is true," or, "If the train arrives in the next five minutes, then it means our love is true." Cassie simultaneously recognized her thoughts and compulsive self-analysis and "tests" were unhelpful but was lost in the fear that she might be making a mistake by participating in this relationship. She reported that she had no concerns about her relationship until after they declared their mutual love and had an argument.

William, a 16-year-old teen, had been dating a girl for six months. He enjoyed spending time with his girlfriend and stated she was a kind, fun and playful person. He enjoyed long conversations and said he could talk with her about anything. He also thought she was attractive, except he thought her breasts were a bit too small. He began obsessing about whether she was sexy enough after some peers joked to him about how he must like his girlfriend for her backside and not her breasts. He was devastated by his intrusive thoughts, "What if I end up being disappointed because her tits are too small?" and had begun avoiding looking at his girlfriend's chest and compulsively checking to make sure he thought her hips, butt and genitals were sufficiently attractive. He also began compulsively asking other males what they thought was sexy about their girlfriends' bodies and became alarmed when someone said they liked everything.

Obsessions and compulsions can become obstacles to a healthy relationship, especially when the patient shares them with their partner either in a misguided attempt to be transparent, or to gain reassurance. More than a few of my patients have caused a premature break-up when they accidentally insult or reject a partner by sharing the content of their obsessions. For example, it can be very painful to be the partner when a patient first declares their love and then later feels compelled to tell you they are not sure they really love you because they notice others. ROCD patients might also repeatedly vacillate between wanting to continue a relationship and wanting to break up to get rid of uncertainty about their feelings. They are typically intolerant of the normal uncertainty that accompanies initial attraction and development of romantic relationships. Here are two examples of typical obsessions and compulsions that can occur in ROCD:

Obsessions	Compulsions
What if I am not properly sexually attracted to my partner?	Checking for sexual arousal, masturbating to check for quality of sexual response to thoughts about the partner, reading about sexual attraction and sexual relationships to obtain reassurance, repeatedly asking the partner to explain how they are sexually attracted to the patient or to others
What if my not liking the moles on their arms means I will never be truly attracted to my partner?	Avoiding looking at moles, scrutinizing emotional response to the idea of moles, asking partner to wear long sleeves, even when making out or at the beach, only making out in the dark
What if our disagreements mean we are doomed?	Avoiding expressing any feelings that might lead to conflict, repeatedly analyzing past disagreements with partner, compulsively reading articles about how to know you have a good relationship, asking others what they think of the relationship and their partner
What if I cannot forget the time they farted, and I will never be able to enjoy them again?	Asking others what they think and feel if their partner farts, reading romantic advice blogs, avoiding partner when feeling overwhelmed by intrusive thoughts, repeatedly reminding partner to avoid farting around them because "It's only polite," not allowing partner to eat gas-producing foods when they are together
What if they are the wrong person because I keep thinking about my other partners?	Repeatedly comparing thoughts about partner with thoughts about other attractive people, repeatedly asking parents and friends how much they think about and notice others who are not their partner
What if I am not really in love because I am sexually attracted to other people?	Repeatedly comparing genital sensations when first sees partner to first seeing others who are attractive, reading media about how to know if the relationship will last, reading about people who cheat and have affairs to conduct a comparison, compulsively asking partner if they think they will be a long-term relationship

ROCD can be challenging in youth because they are in the process of developing romantic partner skills and lack experience and knowledge about the inner workings of attraction, love, sexual bonding and long-term commitment. You need to understand the science behind what is developmentally normal for the process of growing the skills of successful romantic attachment. What might be appropriate in an 11-year-old's style of relationship and attraction would be considered immature in a 15-year-old. For example, an 11 year old might develop a crush on a peer simply because they like the same anime novels and know all the words to the theme song of a favorite show. This would be developmentally normal. A 15-year-old, however, would be expected to be attracted for reasons related to personality and character, in addition to sharing a common interest. Thus, a 15-year-old breaking up with someone because they learned the person liked Brussels sprouts would have different significance than if an 11-year-old made the same decision. Yet, when ROCD enters the zone of romance, this type of black and white thinking can occur and can be difficult to manage unless you have a clear picture of the development of romantic relationship skills and a thorough knowledge of what constitutes successful relationship skills. A further complicating factor is your ability to detect and address cultural myths and customs about romantic relationships that are destructive. ROCD frequently plays off these unhelpful cultural myths and customs to create confusion and impaired romantic experiences. I will discuss each of these important topics so you can have a clear understanding as you sort out your patient's ROCD and help them develop healthy attitudes and skills toward romantic partnership.

ROCD frequently plays off these unhelpful cultural myths and customs to create confusion and impaired romantic experiences.

Healthy development for romantic relationships

The onset of puberty and adolescence includes sexual and romantic attraction that leads to pair bonding. Teens develop interest in romantic and sexual relationships and begin to pursue these interests.

Pre-teens and teens first experience romantic crushes, or immediate strong attractions based on another resembling a romantic or sexual ideal. Early crushes are usually accompanied by a lot of talk with peers, daydreaming and idealization of the object of the crush, but entail little interpersonal engagement. Sitting together at lunch, riding the bus together or sending each other texts is typical. As teens mature, they begin developing attractions that have more basis in interaction, shared interests and shared values. They begin expressing their affection with physical affection or sexual experimentation in addition to developing more realistic expectations and evaluations for who their partner is. They also begin to learn which types of social and emotional interactions work well and which do not. They should discover that the ingredients to successful romantic relationships are primarily the ability to cooperate, be compassionate and forgiving and to communicate thoughtfully and honestly. They should discover that healthy loving relationships involve the ability to love generously, to see the best in one another and to work together, to manage conflict without resorting to defensiveness, contempt, stonewalling or criticism, and respect one another's differences (Gottman & Silver, 2015). This is a great leap from simply finding someone physically attractive or agreeing on taste in music or online games.

Furthermore, most youth who do not have ROCD manage to enter the learning process of crushes, group dating, solo dating and serious relationship commitment with enthusiasm and willingness to take risks. They venture into talking to those they find attractive, dating and attempting various relationships and recognizing that there are no guarantees of success or long-term commitment. They gradually learn through trial and error and observation of peers and parents what elements matter most in romantic relationships. They learn that an attractive appearance has little value unless accompanied by an attractive personality. They learn that everyone is human, has limitations and accidentally disappoints, including themselves. They learn to forgive these disappointments, to distinguish between disappointments that are insignificant and those that matter, such as cheating, theft or aggression. It is hoped that this adolescent process leads to the youth progressing through the three phases of a successful relationship of attraction, building trust and then building long-term commitment based on deep trust and friendship (Gottman & Silver, 2015).

Unfortunately, for patients with ROCD, this uncertain and social risk-taking process of learning is often what triggers obsessions and compulsions. Instead of being able to absorb the lesson, they get stuck on the discrepancy between their idealized view of romance and the reality of human connection. ROCD takes what most consider to be minor events and turns them into worst-case scenarios. I consider ROCD to be what happens when perfectionism about romance becomes entwined with intolerance of uncertainty. The patient typically has some awareness of how their obsessions are unreasonable but lacks the knowledge and experience to undermine the significance of their intrusive thoughts or wants to ditch the relationship or situation to avoid the intrusive thoughts. For example, a patient might prematurely break up with a partner to avoid intrusive thoughts such as, "Is she really the one?" or a patient might begin to defend their OCD intrusive thought about disliking a minor aspect of a partner's appearance when in fact the relationship is mutually satisfying in other ways.

Of special note, ROCD is *not* narcissistic personality disorder or the narcissistic belief that one is entitled to being always pleased and appeased by one's partner. Neither is it the entitled belief that a partner should mold themselves to your every whim. This is uncharacteristic of ROCD. Patients with ROCD maintain an age-appropriate level of empathy for their partners and realize the content of their obsessions would be hurtful to them. For example, one of my university-aged patients developed intrusive thoughts about having made a terrible mistake after he moved in with his long-time girlfriend. He was very distressed because he knew his severe and sudden anxiety that occurred after moving in together was worrying to his girlfriend. He called me in a panic because he did not know how to respond to her questions about the change in his mood for fear of hurting her. He recognized his thinking was anxious, even though he feared it might be indicating something he had missed in evaluating their relationship.

Harmful cultural myths about romance and relationships

Frequently, misunderstanding about the nature of romantic relationships fuels obsessions. For example, if a patient believes true love means never feeling frustration with a partner, then it is easy territory for an obsession to develop once frustration occurs. If a patient believes there is only one perfect partner, then OCD will likely pick at the idea of how to ascertain whether you have found the right one, or will suggest that the normal frustration and conflict a patient feels might mean this partner is not the perfect one. The following is a list of typical myths about romance, love, and sexual attraction that I see fueling intrusive thoughts in my patients:

There is only one perfect partner	You will have no doubts if you truly love someone
If you really love someone, you will feel no attraction to others	If you truly love someone, you will not get really angry or disappointed by them
If you truly love someone, you will constantly feel sexually attracted and ready to have sex	If you truly love someone, you will always want to spend all your time with them and never want alone time or time away from them
If you truly love someone, you will always be smitten by their physical beauty	If you truly love someone, you will have no other priorities that compete with them, such as wanting to complete studies, training or do activities that take away from time with them

It can be helpful to your patients to dispel their myths about romance with information about the science of relationships. If you have not studied the science of successful long-term relationships, you can look in the Resources section for a link to the Gottman Foundation's website that summarizes scientific information about all manner of romantic relationships that has been validated across cultures, continents and sexual orientation. I have compiled the following information to help patients with ROCD who believe in unhelpful romantic myths:

Romantic myth	Factual information
There is only one perfect partner	The most important ingredients for a successful relationship are your partner skills. These can be learned by anyone and best predict who will stay together and who will break up. They are so significant that scientists can predict who will last and who will break up at two years, seven years and much later based on a two-minute video of how a couple solves a problem together
If you love someone, you will always feel in love with them	This only happens during the early, limerence phase of a love relationship. For a relationship to work long term you need to feel deep trust, believe the best of each other, and know how to work well together. Scientists know this is why so many couples break up around two years because this is the longest limerence lasts in the brain
If you truly love someone you will always feel sexually attracted to them and always want to have sex	There is a lot of variety in how much people want to have sex. Changing levels of hormones, fatigue, being too busy, feeling upset and not knowing how to solve conflict can decrease sexual interest. This is normal. Human bodies are not engines designed to always feel and act the same
If you really love someone, you will never feel attraction to others	Puberty turns on your ability to be attracted to others, not just one person. If you really love someone, you choose not to act on your attraction to others
If you truly love someone, you will always be smitten by their beauty	How often do you or your close friends or family look their best, look sexy or look extremely beautiful? Everyone has good hair days and bad hair days, and this is normal. What most people discover is that their attraction is also based on the other person's beautiful character and personality. Thinking someone is attractive is not the same as knowing someone is beautiful inside and out

Taking polls to obtain normative data

You can help patients add to their ammunition against romantic myths by having them take polls from friends and family to obtain normative information about romantic attraction and relationships. I only do this when the patient is not using similar polls as a form of reassurance seeking. Ahead of time, I ask the patient to tell me what they would think if they discovered how others thought about their romantic myths or intrusive thoughts and how they would react if they had a similar thought. Research suggests that most of the population experience intrusive thoughts and consider them a marker of stress or a quirky idea to be ignored (Barrera & Norton, 2011). You can create an analogous thought that resembles the patient's intrusive thought to make it easier for them to query others. Patients can do this through a group text chat, on a public forum or in person. Before the patient conducts the poll, I ask them to think like a scientist and to decide ahead of time what different results would indicate. For example, if only two out of 30 people agreed with their romantic myth, would that show support for their myth being the way most people think and operate? This part is important because you are trying to get them to test the faulty hypothesis of their OCD. Patients can startle when they find one person who agrees with their unhelpful fear. You need to counter the emotional reasoning that accompanies a response that agrees with OCD.

These are some examples of poll questions:

1. Do you believe there is only one person in the universe for you and you are out of luck if you never meet them? Or do you believe that there are probably many people who could make a great partner?

2. Can a person sometimes think their partner is unattractive or not looking their best when they are in love with them?

3. Can people who are in love and have a great relationship have conflict or arguments or times of not getting along?

4. Can you be sexually attracted to someone without being in love with them?

5. Can you fantasize about other people even when you are in a great relationship?

6. Can you lose your interest in sex even when you love someone or believe they are sexy?

Imaginal exposure for ROCD

Imaginal exposure should target the patient's worst-case scenario. You can either do this in a graduated fashion or have the patient randomly select different worst-case words, phrases or thoughts to practice. Random selection better mimics what happens outside the therapist's office and increases resilience, but some patients are not willing to begin with this strategy. In this case, I begin with graduated exposure and advance to random exposure as the patient gains confidence in their ability to confront their anxiety. You can have the patients list fear-provoking words, phrases and sentences or tell elaborate worst-case stories that reflect their obsessions. The goal is to learn to tolerate the intrusive thought without giving in to the urge to seek reassurance, avoid or do compulsions. Here is an example of how Charlotte did imaginal exposure for her ROCD:

Therapist: "Charlotte, your OCD keeps suggesting you do not really love your boyfriend each time you feel less than perfectly in love with him. We have already talked about how impossible it is to always feel perfectly in love with someone, and we know that everything seems to be going fine with your relationship other than that OCD keeps making you wonder whether you are truly in love. It's time to help you get used to your intrusive thoughts so you can learn to give them less attention. What are some of the scary things your OCD says?"

Charlotte: "What if I don't really love him? What if I am not supposed to be with him? What if I never feel at peace with loving him?"

Therapist: "Those are great examples of scary thoughts. Let's repeat them back and forth. You copy what I say and repeat it five times in a row. Ready? What if I never figure out if I love him? What if I never know for sure? Now repeat that five times."

Charlotte whispers these phrases five times.

Therapist: "Let's see if you can do that again, only louder, like you want me to hear."

Charlotte repeats the phrases with a louder voice.

Therapist: "Fantastic! I am so proud of you because I know that is difficult. Let's keep doing this and see how long it takes for it to feel easier to say these phrases."

After repeating these phrases for ten minutes, Charlotte indicates that it is getting easier to say them.

Therapist: "What did you just learn when you kept repeating those phrases over and over instead of trying to prove them wrong or right? Instead of getting reassurance?"

Charlotte: "I can do it! I thought I would die of anxiety if I did what we just did."

Therapist: "So, it sounds as if you are discovering that you are stronger than OCD and stronger than you once thought?"

Charlotte: "Yes!"

Therapist: "Well, let's get even stronger and make this a little more difficult. How about you repeat after me and see if you can make it even more difficult by adding in more scary ideas? Can you do that to push back against your OCD?"

Charlotte nods yes.

Therapist: "Here we go: 'I will never find true love. Something is wrong and I will never be able to find true love.' Now, your turn."

Charlotte repeats the phrases and adds in: "I will be unhappy forever and never get married and be the only one who is single among my friends."

Exposure and response prevention practice

For most patients, exposure practice will entail confrontation of feared intrusive thoughts and ideas along with eliminating any reassurance seeking or checking for emotional or sexual response. Some patients, however, will also need exposure to behaviors they have been avoiding or to situations they have been avoiding. Patients may avoid looking at others for fear of noticing feelings of attraction, may not look at certain parts of their partner's body, may dim the lights to avoid looking or may avoid sexual arousal for fear it isn't enough or isn't the right quality. My guideline for determining how to conduct exposure in these instances where the patient is avoiding age-appropriate desired sexual or romantic behavior is to ask the patient what they wish they could do if they did not have OCD. I also take into consideration family or religious values, the local culture, and the advisability of the behavior in question. My preference is for young teens to delay sexual relationships until they are more mature because research shows early onset of sexual activity is associated with school dropout, early pregnancy and sexually transmitted diseases, all of which jeopardize teens' mental and physical health (Zimmer-Gembeck & Helfand, 2008). Here is an example of exposure with response prevention after first doing imaginal exposure and practice in delaying mental checking rituals (see the previous chapter for an explanation of this technique).

CASE EXAMPLE

Gregory, a 17-year-old, was avoiding having sex so that he didn't have to notice a part of his partner's body, the sight of which triggered intrusive thoughts. When he saw his partner's belly which was slightly pudgy, he got the thought, "What if you do not really think they are sexy? What if you think they are ugly and lose your erection? What if this means you shouldn't be together?" Since he had been involved in a previous romantic relationship that included sex, I explained how his OCD was hijacking his relationship and sex life.

Therapist: "It looks as if your OCD is interfering with your ability to enjoy your partner and even to have sex. Unfortunately, the more you avoid something, the more anxiety you create, and the more you will create feelings that are incompatible with feeling aroused and interested in sex. In fact, if you hope to enjoy sex, you do best if you are just feeling and enjoying sensations instead of thinking about them. So, let's come up with some ideas for getting cuddlier with your partner. How about these ideas: holding hands, hugging or leaning your head on their shoulder for starters, and doing this in broad daylight? Would you be willing to try this?"

Gregory: "I might, but what if I get stuck having obsessions? What if they want to do more?"

Therapist: "Remember how the imaginal exposure practice you have been doing and the practice focusing on the present moment once you get thoughts has helped you decrease mental checking about how you respond to thinking about your partner? You have done so well at this that I think you are ready to try exposure with your partner. I think you might be surprised at what happens when you try. You are much better at encountering your intrusive thoughts and not giving in to mental rituals. Now you need to get rid of your avoidance while avoiding doing rituals when it comes to being with your partner."

Once Gregory was able to do these exposure tasks with a high degree of response prevention, we discussed kissing and making out. He was anxious about doing this because he feared failure, so we redefined failure and success.

Therapist: "Failure is letting your OCD be the dictator of your love life. If you do not take risks and try following your heart, then you have let OCD win in the battle for control over your life. Success is doing any exposure task no matter what. Success is taking risks to take back control by allowing yourself to learn. No one gets it right when they are learning. Do you remember when you told me how your first kiss felt? Strange and not what you expected? That shows how sexual behavior is something we all must learn. You are just going to have to learn again how to kiss and enjoy your partner because OCD got in the way. So, making the effort is the success, especially if you do get intrusive thoughts. The only way you will get confident in managing your OCD is by doing it. I know that if you can keep practicing using ERP, then you will learn to have fun."

One area of response prevention that deserves special mention is the use of digital devices to do reassurance seeking and checking. Many patients look at blogs, magazines and websites for information about love, sexual attraction and romance. They can also access porn to verify their sexual response and degree of attraction, or track the relationships of others to gain reassurance about what others think, feel and do. When this occurs in response to OCD-driven anxiety, as opposed to general curiosity, it is never helpful. Additionally, teens who spend a lot of time viewing and masturbating to pornography may curtail their ability to respond freely to a partner who has no surgical or photoshopped enhancements and who does not use suggestive talk designed to generate money or extended viewing time (Camilleri, Perry & Sammut, 2020; Mattebo *et al.*, 2018). You may need to find ways to block websites or alone time with digital devices early in treatment to help secure response prevention. Most smartphones, computers and digital devices have a parental control setting that can both block content and turn off the device during pre-designated hours. I have found this to be helpful when patients acknowledge they need help controlling their digital access to content they might use for reassurance seeking. You can also obtain inexpensive flip phones that allow texting but no internet surfing so your patient can have social access while preventing opportunities for digital reassurance seeking. My goal is to set the stage for success during the early stages of treatment when it is most difficult to develop the habit of saying "No" to compulsive digital searches. I fade out the digital security as the patient demonstrates skill in avoiding the temptation to respond to intrusive thoughts with compulsions.

Next, I will discuss assessing and treating obsessions about self-harm and harming others.

If you would like to view a demonstration of how to implement some of the strategies mentioned in this chapter, please go to https://library.jkp.com/redeem using the code ZVEAZDD.

CHAPTER 9

Treating Self-Harm and Harming OCD

Suicidal, Self-Injury and Harming Obsessions and Compulsions

Global increases in the rates of suicidal ideation, suicide attempts and completions, and self-injury have made the task of risk assessment for self-harm more prevalent in the minds of mental health professionals (Shobhana & Raviraj, 2022; Ruch *et al.*, 2019). Furthermore, increases in overall rates of mental illness in youth and the alarming phenomenon of the willingness of some youth to attempt mass shootings in the United States have created a valid concern for mental health professionals to detect and prevent attempts at self-harm and harm to others. The assumption for many is that poor mental health is associated with risk for suicide and harm to others. The dilemma for clinicians is that the science underlying accurate assessment and prevention is a relatively new topic for research and our ability to intervene reflects our lack of knowledge (McCoy, 2022; Lowe & Galea, 2017; Cabrera & Kwon, 2018; Cornell *et al.*, 2022). This adds an element of uncertainty and risk taking for any clinician who encounters patients who mention self-harm, suicide or harming others. A further complication is the way your professional community understands and handles risk. For example, in my nearby community, several schools refer for immediate mental health evaluation any student who mentions self-harm or suicide in any manner. This means students who write poems or stories about suicidal actions get referred along with students who text their friends about wanting to die. Additionally, some schools call the police for any student who mentions wanting to kill someone, but do not first refer them for mental health evaluation. Likewise, I have been referred children as young as seven for evaluation for mental health or dangerousness when they wrote stories about killing other people. Other schools appear to have a higher tolerance for risk and typically do not refer students for creative writing assignments that cover distressing topics and feel able to handle students who get angry in a fight and tell someone else they wish they were dead. The problem for clinicians is managing their own response to the lower risk tolerance of others. If you are prone to anxiety or worry, or pride yourself on being very conservative, then you might accidentally find yourself agreeing with your patient's OCD when it expresses concern about harm to self or others. Our instinct as humans is to first pay attention to fear signals and this includes the fear signals others give when they fear for a patient's safety or for the safety of other potential victims. Sadly, I was once referred a seven-year-old boy for assessment of possible predatory sexual behavior because he told a teacher he was afraid he touched a girl's private parts. The school had a social worker assess him for history of sexual abuse or sexually inappropriate behavior and then, fearful of making a mistake or risking a lawsuit, the social worker called child protective services and me, when there was no good reason to suspect anything other than anxiety about doing the wrong thing. All the professional attention and questions made the patient even more anxious, more obsessed about causing harm and further increased his compulsive confessions and reassurance seeking. He misunderstood everyone's attention as evidence confirming his OCD's worst fears, that he would lose control and inappropriately touch someone.

Here is a similar example of professional difficulty tolerating risk gone awry. I frequently see teens who get intrusive thoughts about suicide or self-harm, who are aghast at the idea of self-harming or completing suicide but feel compelled to tell parents and counselors as a compulsive way to gain reassurance they are not at risk. Frequently, these patients are sent to the Emergency Department or therapists for assessment of risk to self. Although they are typically never hospitalized, it creates a pattern that either reinforces the validity of the intrusive thoughts, "What if I kill myself? What if I cut myself?" and introduces the notion that the best and only way to get reassurance is to go to the Emergency Department and have multiple specialists decide there is no risk. It becomes a lengthy and expensive ritual of reassurance seeking that increases intolerance of uncertainty. It also tends to make the parents and school staff believe this is necessary, even when they think that the child is not really at risk because they have never acted on their intrusive thoughts.

Lastly, I have worked with students who got intrusive thoughts about mass shooting or mass murder, largely in part because this is now part of the news cycle that triggers the initial worst-case obsession, "What if I am a mass murderer? What if I someday get a gun and kill everyone and get shot by the police?" Unfortunately, some of these students have had the same response from the school system of being referred to the Emergency Department, to therapy or, even more triggering for their OCD, the police. Inappropriate referral to the police ends up being traumatic and reifying intrusive thoughts. No school or therapist wants to be the one who mistakenly overlooks a potential mass murderer.

Similarly, I have treated young men with OCD who get intrusive thoughts about having non-consensual sex because both they and their partner had been drinking or their partner changed their mind during sex, ended sexual activities, or they encountered women who believed the power differential of white male privilege or male privilege prevents women from granting consent. How then do you proceed to manage this type of OCD that focuses on content all agree is egregious or dangerous without getting caught in the trap of lowering your threshold for uncertainty to preserve your credentials and professional ethics while doing no harm to the patient?

Differential diagnosis

One of the most important things to know about the harming subtype of OCD is that it is inversely associated with violence to self and others (Brakoulias *et al.*, 2013; Lundström *et al.*, 2014; Rahman, Webb & Wittkowski, 2021). The patients who have this variant of OCD are the people least likely to commit the violence they imagine. Their problem is they fear their intrusive thoughts and mistake them as evidence of their behavioral potential for violence. They are particularly bothered by the phenomenon of thought-action fusion, discussed at the beginning of Chapter 2. Patients falsely believe that if they can imagine self-harm or harm to others, then it must indicate that they have an unknown or unrecognized desire and ability to commit real harm. For example, a six-year-old girl has obsessions about pulling off her cat's tail and then begins to avoid touching the cat's tail, then touching the cat at all and compulsively confesses, "I might have hurt the cat's tail, Mummy." A pre-teen gets obsessions about having oral sex with their younger siblings and pets. They then do compulsive research about molestors and avoid all physical contact with siblings and pets and compulsively review their memories for evidence of inappropriate touching so much they cannot get enough sleep. The fact that the patient would rather not think about the intrusive thoughts and wants to protect themselves and others from harm is their insurance against committing harm. Another example is of a young adult who gets intrusive thoughts about rude people, "They should die!", and pictures a torturous death.

> *Patients falsely believe that if they can imagine self-harm or harm to others, then it must indicate that they have an unknown or unrecognized desire and ability to commit real harm.*

They feel horrified by their thoughts and compulsively attempt to undo their intrusive thoughts by thinking good thoughts about rude people. They falsely believe they should not feel anger toward others and should never imagine anything other than nice things happening to others. They confuse the feeling of wanting revenge with the actual act of getting revenge: thought-action fusion. Thus, there are several questions that are very important to ask when a patient discloses thoughts about harm:

1. Are you afraid that having these thoughts might make you act on these thoughts?

2. Are you worried that these thoughts will make you become the kind of person you do not want to be?

3. What is the worst thing about having these thoughts? (If the answer is some version of "They might make me do something terrible," then it is OCD.)

4. What would you think of someone if they had the same kind of thoughts even though they did not believe in the thoughts? (If they indicate that they believe the person would be dangerous or undesirable, then it is OCD.)

Youth who do not have OCD do not fear their ugly or violent intrusive thoughts and they do not consider them to be dangerous in others. They view them as the product of stress or a vivid imagination. What they do worry about is people who have the intention and motivation to harm themselves or others. They recognize the distinction between imagining something awful, even in revenge, and truly desiring something awful to occur. They also recognize that intention is an important part of morality, and they distinguish between accidental harm and intended harm. Patients with thought-action fusion confuse thinking about something ahead of time or accidentally doing something that might lead to harm (e.g. bumping into someone's genital area after worrying about not bumping into someone's genital area) with wanting to commit harm and taking action to create harm. This is an important distinction, because treatment often entails helping young OCD patients to learn about this distinction so they can more readily have insight into the unhelpful effects of their OCD. Thus, a child without OCD might find it delicious to imagine torture to another child who just pushed them out of line, while a child with harming OCD might feel mortified and do compulsions should their angry imagination think the same thought of revenge, despite having no intention of taking vengeful action.

Additionally, patients who suffer from both harming OCD and true suicidal ideation and suicidal attempts will be able to distinguish between the two types of thoughts, with the distinction being that obsessions make them anxious and the idea of suicide seems like a relief or a way to escape the pain of living.

Neutralizing behaviors disguised as harming behaviors

Some patients attempt to get rid of their obsessions by doing the forbidden thing, such as touching someone on their butt, placing a knife on their wrist or looking at sexual images of children. This may seem contradictory unless you understand the motivation behind the behavior to rid oneself of uncertainty. When patients do this, they are trying to get rid of the uncertainty about harming self or others by "getting it over with" in a false belief that this will neutralize or stop the intrusive thoughts once and for all. They might also seek reassurance by testing themselves to see if they feel agreement with the intrusive thoughts. This typically occurs as a desperate, last-effort compulsion after previous avoidance, reassurance seeking and compulsions have failed to bring relief from the intrusive thoughts and anxiety. At no time does the patient endorse or desire the obsession of harm. They feel disgust and alarm at the idea of harm. Frequently, their explanation for why they did the thing they abhor is, "I just couldn't stand the thoughts anymore. I thought if I went ahead and touched someone's ass, then I would know for sure if I was a gay predator," or, "I didn't want to die. I was so scared my thoughts about suicide were real and I thought if I scratched my wrists then I would know for sure if they were real," or, "I don't really want to molest babies, but I can't get rid of these thoughts. I just felt like I must be a molester and if I touched the baby then I would know whether I would lose control." Each of these thoughts illustrates the desire to gain certainty even though the patient clearly understands the behavior is distasteful or criminal. The anxiety about wanting to verify their potential for harm is the motivation, as opposed to a desire to gain emotional anesthesia or engage in non-consensual sexual contact. Unfortunately, in cases like these, the tendency for parents and mental health professionals is to become alarmed and assume the same fear as the patient's OCD. Risk-assessment interviews that fail to assess for harming OCD can generate some confusing responses from these patients as they grill the patient for their true intention and awareness of the inappropriateness of their compulsive behavior. If you have ever questioned a patient who has doubt and intolerance of uncertainty about their thoughts and behavior, you know how circular and confusing the conversation can become, which accidentally pushes the patient into more doubt and the mistaken assumption that they truly are dangerous. Let me illustrate a typical unhelpful interview:

Therapist: "Your parents told me you were touching your baby sister's private parts and said you admitted you did it on purpose. What made you want to touch her that way?"

Patient: "I get these thoughts. I know they are bad, but they keep happening. I keep thinking about her vagina. I know it was wrong, but I touched her. Do you think I am a child molester?"

Therapist: "We'll talk about that later. What kind of thoughts do you get?"

Patient: "I keep thinking I should lick her and do oral sex. Is something wrong with me?"

Therapist: "I don't know if something is wrong with you. Do you think it's okay to lick your sister that way? Or do you think that is something only adults should do when they love each other?"

Patient: "Am I sick? Are you going to send me to one of those homes for bad children? Is my sister going to be okay?"

Therapist: "Do you think you will ever touch your sister that way again?"

Patient: "I don't know! What if I do it again? Do you think I am a monster?"

Now, let's contrast this with a different kind of interview in which the therapist is enlightened about OCD:

Therapist: "Your parents told me you touched your baby sister's private parts and have been worrying a lot about whether you are a bad person who wants to have sex with babies. Some kids think that is the scariest worst thought in the world and wish they never thought those thoughts and some kids think those thoughts feel interesting even though they know others might not like those thoughts. Does either one of those sound like you?"

Patient: "I hate my thoughts! I wish I had never touched her. Do you think I am a child molester?"

Therapist: "I am going to ask a few more questions about what happened before I give you an answer. It sounds as if you get super anxious when you get these thoughts. Do you ever do anything to try and get rid of these thoughts or to make it so they won't happen?"

Patient: "I try not to look at my sister and I try not to be the one that helps with her diaper or dressing her. I try to make myself think good things and remind myself how much I love my sister. I pray to God to protect my sister and make sure no one molests her."

Mother: "She is always asking us if we think she is a good person or if she is ever the type of person who will go to jail someday. She even asks us silly questions like, 'Can people be sent to jail if they are not sure they committed a crime?'"

Therapist: "It sounds as if your thoughts terrify you, like many other kids I have seen. Sometimes kids who get thoughts like yours get so fed up with their thoughts and trying to figure out what they mean they do things, like touching a sister, to see for sure if they really are a bad person. Does that sound like you? Were you hoping to see if you somehow were a molester by touching your sister? Like trying to see if you really liked molesting her?"

Patient: "Yes, I just couldn't take the thoughts anymore and I felt that if I touched her then somehow the thoughts would go away. If I didn't like it then I would know for sure what I am. You've seen this in other kids before?"

Therapist: "Yes, I have. You are not alone, and it sounds like your real problem is OCD. Do you want to know why I think that?"

The important distinction you are trying to assess is the patient's motivation for doing the undesirable behavior and the presence of anxiety about the intrusive thoughts and the uncertainty they generate. It is the same phenomenon you assess for all obsessions and compulsions. What causes anxiety and doubt and what mental or behavioral actions are deployed to alleviate anxiety and doubt? Young people with OCD will be on a mission to eliminate anxiety and doubt, regardless of the content of their obsessions and compulsions. Young people who are suicidal will be motivated to permanently end emotional pain and/or avoid overwhelming shame. Young people who engage in self-harm will be motivated to gain momentary relief from emotional pain. Young people who harm others will be motivated to gain revenge, seek thrills or gain sexual thrills. When you focus on the function of the thoughts and behavior then you can more accurately assess any patient, especially those with OCD whose content is alarming.

Explaining harmful compulsive behaviors

When a patient has done inappropriate things to neutralize their OCD, it is very important to help them, their parents and any other people involved to understand the diagnosis and how this differs from things that are truly risky. One of the first things to address is the meaning of the patient's compulsive attempt to neutralize intrusive thoughts. This is important because everyone is typically haunted by the patient's act, fearing it will happen again or that even worse might occur. If a patient is especially impulsive, for example has attention deficit hyperactivity disorder or executive functioning difficulties, then they may need more supervision or barriers to prevent the harmful compulsion until their OCD is better managed. My experience has been that this group of young people are the ones more likely to engage in this type of compulsion when it occurs, perhaps because they are more impulsive. Here is how I try to explain what happens:

> Therapist: "Having OCD is like walking across a balance beam without falling or trying to ride your bicycle on a line without swerving. It seems that the more you think about falling or

swerving, the more likely you are to get wobbly and fall off the beam or swerve off the line. You don't want to fall or swerve, but because you think so much about the thing you do not want to do, you accidentally do it even though you do not want to.

"When patients want to get rid of unwanted thoughts, they are very afraid having the thoughts means they are a bad person. Why on earth would a good person think such awful thoughts? They do not realize that everyone else gets the same thoughts. They get so worried they want to know for sure if the bad thoughts mean they are a bad person. So, they do an experiment to try and make things go one way or the other, so they know for sure. The only problem is that OCD always makes it harder. Once you do something, then OCD comes back and says even though you did not like it, the fact that you did it means you must really be bad. Then you are back at the start all over again because OCD will never let you win. That's why getting rid of the thoughts always backfires."

Once I feel confident the parents, patient and others understand the diagnosis, I then take precautions, such as removing sharp objects from view if cutting happened in response to OCD, supervising inter-actions in which inappropriate touching occurred or monitoring other relevant situations. This measure is temporary. I explain to everyone that these measures will be removed at the appropriate time when exposure practice permits and I encourage exposure to the same situations using response prevention. I make sure that everyone knows that this is for the purpose of preventing compulsive behaviors as opposed to protecting from harm. This is an important distinction.

Compulsive confessing and false memories

Some patients manage their intolerance of uncertainty by repeatedly recalling situations in which they fear they might have committed a harming act. Initially they recall this memory of a near encounter to determine whether they did the act they fear. Unfortunately, they are also simultaneously worrying about doing the thing they fear.

Constant repetition with high levels of anxiety then blends the two ideas, the actual memory of a near miss with the act itself (e.g. sweeping food into the opening of the garbage disposal with a hand while it is grinding food, with the idea of placing one's hand into the grinder). This repetition and a desire for certainty create the phenomenon of a false memory the patient becomes convinced is true and assumes to be evidence of their potential for harm. They react to the false memory as though it is a real memory, even though there is no objective evidence to suggest they put themselves or others in peril.

False memories occur when a person repeatedly imagines something to be true that never occurred. Elizabeth Loftus's research shows the surprising ease with which a person can create a false memory when they, or others, assume an imagined scenario is true (Loftus, 1996). For example, a therapist can accidentally assume a patient has been sexually assaulted and repeatedly imply or state that the patient's nightmares have content indicative of night-time sexual assault by an alcoholic father. The patient then confabulates a false memory. Or a friend could repeatedly recall an event the patient never attended but tell the patient they were present, and the patient then recalls the memory as though they were present. This explains false eyewitness reports and the anxiety-provoking phenomenon of harming OCD patients falsely feeling convinced they did something unacceptable.

The natural response for many people to the knowledge of doing something unforgivable is to seek forgiveness through confession. Harming OCD patients, in this case, are attempting to repair a supposed moral failing instead of just seeking reassurance. They want absolution from significant others, the therapist, themselves and often the supposed victim. This can create a perplexing dilemma when patients turn themselves in for harm they did not commit, such as informing an authority they ran over a pedestrian, telling a counselor they sexually assaulted a child they babysat or telling a counselor they sexually assaulted someone at a drunken university party. Typically, these confessions end up puzzling those who hear them because the patient's recounting lacks details that suggest harm occurred. Unfortunately, each compulsive confession reifies the belief that the false memory is real.

Additionally, patients who accidentally create false memories are likely to have a scrupulous quality to their mindset about morality that makes it difficult to forgive or accept inadvertent human action that might lead to harm. They view awareness of harm and accidental harm (e.g. accidentally bumping into a passerby while knowing they might stumble into oncoming traffic and be killed) as the same as deliberate murder. When this occurs, you should use the techniques in Chapter 4 to help your patient build self-compassion and the ability to forgive themselves.

Imaginal exposure

Typical obsessions focus on inflicting harm on oneself or others. They can be triggered by news or awareness of a suicide, self-injury or violence committed against others. Patients might read a story about suicide, learn mental health information about self-harm and suicidal thoughts or hear shocking news reports of interpersonal violence or mass violence. Here is a sample list of harming obsession and compulsions:

Obsessions	Compulsions
What if I stab myself in the eye?	Avoiding pencils, pens, anything sharp, keeping hands away from eyes, sleeping with hands underneath body, wearing sunglasses
Pushing a pedestrian into the traffic	Avoiding walking by other pedestrians, holding hands in pockets when walking in school hallways, riding bicycle instead of riding the bus to avoid the bus queue
Killing myself by hanging	Getting rid of belts, refusing to wear a tie or hoodie string, refusing to wear anything snug around neck, sleeping on top of bedding to avoid accidental choking on bedsheets
Raping my parents	Locking bedroom door at night, insisting parents lock theirs, avoiding looking at parents and being at home, refusing to touch parents, sitting as far away as possible from parents
Molesting small children	Refusing to be around small children, giving up babysitting jobs, analyzing past memories for evidence of accidental molestation, refusing to look at small children or talk about children

cont.

Obsessions	Compulsions
Killing everyone at school	Avoiding all media about mass violence, guns, warfare, violence, excessive compulsive kindness and thoughtful behaviors, avoiding walking too close to others to avoid touching them or bumping them, refusing to read history assignments about warfare, repeatedly asking parents if they think they will do great good in the future

Imaginal exposure must focus on the feared thoughts, no matter how gruesome or inappropriate. Some therapists fear doing this type of exposure because they mistakenly believe focusing on these ideas will increase the likelihood of the patient acting on these ideas. This assumption is incorrect and belies the diagnosis of OCD. It also overlooks the ubiquitous nature of intrusive thoughts (Barrera & Norton, 2011) that shows these unpleasant and gruesome thoughts to be universal. Awareness of harm is not the critical and causal factor for harm to occur. Thus, imaginal exposure for harming OCD should address the words, ideas and scenarios feared by each patient. I start first with imaginal exposure because the bulk of the patient's OCD is driven by fear of intrusive thoughts. I also ask the patient to refrain from avoidance, reassurance seeking and other compulsions once we begin imaginal exposure. Here are some ideas for imaginal exposure:

1. Writing down words, then phrases, then sentences that are feared.

2. Drawing pictures of feared scenes, body parts, weapons or other dangerous objects or situations.

3. Selecting cartoons, then photos, then videos of items that trigger fear, such as knives, guns, rope, underwear, bathing suits, gravestones.

4. Watching feared photos or videos on a small phone screen then working up to a larger computer screen or television screen that has bigger images.

5. Writing stories depicting the terrible events happening with all the terrible consequences.

6. Reading or saying aloud terrible stories.

7. Listening to parents and therapist explain how the patient really manifests what OCD fears.

8. Reading media about youth who do the things the patient fears.

Managing graphic content

Sometimes your patient's intrusive thoughts will be graphic with explicit sexual or violent content, so much so that it would be inappropriate to look at depictions or play videos matching this content. In this instance, I refrain from matching the content of their OCD in the search for images or videos and instead find images that trigger the patient's intrusive thoughts and ask them to elaborate on what they see by making the imagery in their mind what their OCD fears. For example, I might have a teen who fears raping peers look at a yearbook, social media or school websites that show peers and then ask them to imagine abducting and raping the person they see. This mimics the activity of the OCD while allowing you to practice using exposure and response prevention. Another example would be to have a patient who fears murdering and mutilating pets look at websites about cute puppies and point out all the ways she would torture and murder each pet she sees without avoiding, getting reassurance or doing other compulsions.

Taking surveys

You can have the patient take surveys of their peers or others to find out how common intrusive thoughts are in the general population. As mentioned in the previous chapter, this exercise helps build insight into OCD and the ability to dismiss the thoughts as meaningless. When giving this assignment, I instruct patients to ask others, "I am taking a survey to see what kinds of weird thoughts everyone gets. Would you be willing to help me?" Then I give them a checklist of intrusive thoughts that cover the patient's category, as well as others, with a checkbox beside it, so the participant does not have to list their specific thought. Here is a sample:

Please put a check by any weird thoughts you have had that you did not agree with:

- ❑ Hurting someone with a sharp object when I did not want to

- ❑ Pushing someone into the street or off a bridge when I did not want to

- ❑ Jumping off a bridge or out of a window when I did not want to

- ❑ Hurting myself or killing myself when I did not want to

- ❑ Destroying someone or something when I did not want to

- ❑ Having sex with someone/an animal when I did not want to

- ❑ Hurting myself with a sharp object, hanging or burning when I did not want to

- ❑ Torturing someone or a pet when I did not want to

Once you get the survey results, which will always indicate that others share similar thoughts, you can ask the patient what this means about their thoughts. Are they really unusual or indicative of potential for harm, or are they just disturbing to think about?

Exposure practice

Reassurance seeking is one of the most common rituals associated with harming OCD. Patients who are younger frequently ask parents for reassurance they are a good person or for confirmation they are not a bad person. They might also ask if their thoughts will come true or request that adults make promises that intrusive thoughts are untrue. Older children might ask for reassurance but are more likely to attempt to hide their intrusive thoughts due to shame and embarrassment, and their reassurance seeking is more likely to involve a romantic partner or best friend, if at all. Their reassurance-seeking rituals are more likely to be private activities, such as reading about criminals and comparing their characteristics with the criminals. When reassurance seeking involves others, I insist these people become involved in treatment. I ask them to respond to the patient's requests for reassurance by giving them a statement to repeat so they can avoid getting entangled in a reassurance-seeking conversation. I give them these two choices, one of which allows them to blame the therapist for failing to provide reassurance and one of which increases uncertainty for the patient:

"Looks as if your OCD is making you ask that question. It's doctor's orders that I do not reply."

"Looks as if your OCD is making you ask that question. I cannot say anything one way or the other."

I have the patient practice seeking reassurance while the parents use these two responses, being sure to have the patient pretend to cry, get angry or have a tantrum. Patients earn rewards for quietly accepting a non-reassuring response from the parents, and parents are instructed to walk away and ignore the patient after they give the initial response, as opposed to repeating the response or trying to persuade the child to cooperate.

When reassurance seeking takes the form of internet searches for information about sexual predators, mass murderers and so on, I implement parental controls to eliminate compulsive surfing and ask the patient to repeat their imaginal exposure instead. I make the point that ERP is the fastest way to get rid of OCD, not reassurance seeking. I record imaginal exposure practice from the session and assign it to the patient to repeat every day.

I also have patients post triggering pictures and words in their bedroom, on their smartphone and on their walls. I make sure other family members have an accurate understanding of the person's OCD and know they are to leave these exposure triggers alone for the benefit of the patient. I avoid posting anything that would prove to be embarrassing or criminal but stick to things such as children in swimsuits for those who fear pedophilic thoughts, or pictures of lethal combat knives for those who fear stabbing others or themselves. The patient's goal is to repeatedly encounter these images and ideas while not doing anything to avoid or undo their intrusive thoughts.

In vivo exposure practice

Harming OCD patients need to encounter all the situations they avoid or endure with the reassurance of rituals and reassurance seeking. This often includes being in situations that might initially appear to be awkward or uncomfortable. The idea is to create the situations people naturally encounter that trigger OCD. For example, when a patient fears committing sexual violence and avoids looking at others, they need to do exposure by looking. If they avoid being near certain people, they need to practice getting close or even accidentally touching these people. If they avoid using sharp objects for fear of stabbing them-selves, then they need to practice using sharp objects and act as though they will stab themselves for the sake of exposure practice. If they fear they will lose control and stab someone, they need to practice wielding a knife behind your back while you look away. Let me illustrate how this is done with a child who fears stabbing her family and pets:

Therapist: "You have done a great job with your imaginal expo-sure Now it's time to increase the challenge and build your skill in pushing back OCD. I want you to do what I do. We each have a big knife that is sharp. Do you think this could kill someone?"

Patient: "Yes! This knife is too big. I cannot believe you are going to make me hold it."

Therapist: "I know you are ready to hold it. Your OCD is the one who believes it is too dangerous to hold. Now let's pick it up like this (therapist holds the knife by the handle, pointing it toward the floor). Good, that's the way to hold it."

Patient: "This knife is so big! Are you sure this is safe? I thought adults weren't supposed to give kids knives."

Therapist: "If you lived 40 years ago you would always carry a pocketknife, so let's see who is right, OCD or me. Do you feel that holding this knife is making you want to burst loose and become a psycho knife killer or are you just getting scary thoughts?"

Patient: "Just scary thoughts. Are you sure this is okay?"

Therapist: "Just copy me (starts to wave the knife back and forth with the blade pointing toward each other, and the patient copies movement). Good. That is a nice wave. It looks like one of those villains who is getting ready to stab someone in a fight, don't you think?"

Patient: "Don't say that! What if it slips from my hands?"

Therapist: "Well, let's see if it slips from your hands or mine and find out how dangerous that is. What is your OCD saying now?"

Patient: "It's telling me that this is super dangerous and I should stop. What if I hurt you?"

Therapist: "You are doing a terrific job! I am so proud of you. Did you ever think you would be waving a butcher's knife like this? What does this tell you about who is stronger? You or your OCD?"

Patient: "I am stronger, but I am so scared!"

Therapist: "Yes, you are stronger. Brilliant insight. Being scared is the sign that we are doing the best exposure. What would make this even scarier?"

Patient: "If I sit closer to you."

Therapist: "Great idea! Let's do it (the therapist moves closer to the patient). Keep waving your knife like this (demonstrates waving and jabbing the knife, which the patient copies). Now, let's make it even better practice by saying, 'What if I lose control and stab you?' (the patient and therapist each repeat this phrase while waving and jabbing the knives). Now, what would your OCD think if you wave your knife while I put mine down so I am defenseless?"

The previous illustration shows how to progress through various exposure practices while encouraging the patient, reinforcing them for handling their anxiety and increasing the level of difficulty while avoiding giving reassurance. When patients ask for reassurance during a session, I initially give one explanation on the first question and then explain that I will not answer any future reassurance-seeking questions, so I do not accidentally make their OCD worse. I often just ignore the question and redirect the patient to the exposure task. When this does not work, I remind them how their OCD is attempting to destroy their success. I might say, "Looks as if your OCD is trying to make you get reassurance. That is so frustrating because it's just another way for your OCD to keep you from getting rid of it and enjoying a fun life. Doing your practice right now is the best way to fight back. You must practice not knowing for sure in order to push back against OCD."

Here are examples of exposure exercises you can use with harming OCD:

Compulsion	Exposure practice
Avoiding small children for fear of becoming a pedophile	Going to playgrounds with small children and talking to the children, babysitting, helping small children dress and bathe, changing a diaper, banning compulsive confessions of false memories of abuse or inappropriate touching
Avoiding locker rooms and looking at peers for fear of sexually molesting peers	Visiting public locker rooms and counting the number of boxers vs briefs, or thongs vs bikinis, counting the number of necklaces girls wear, elastic waist vs belted waist, button vs zip fly on jeans, pockets vs no pockets on pants and shorts, bikinis vs one-piece bathing costumes
Avoiding sharp objects and being near anyone when using a pencil or pen	Slicing food or cutting shapes while near others, handing others knives and scissors, holding pencils and pens like weapons and stabbing the air with them toward others, standing behind others and wielding sharp objects while repeating feared phrases
Avoiding pets for fear of torturing and molesting small animals	Playing with pets, visiting a pet shelter and walking dogs, holding sharp objects near pets, holding ropes near pets, tying a scarf around a pet's neck, putting pet clothing on pet while saying feared phrases

cont.

Compulsion	Exposure practice
Avoiding sharp objects for fear of killing oneself or stabbing oneself in the eye	Holding knives, scissors and pencils near eyes, waving them near eyes, repeating feared phrases while holding sharp objects near eyes
Avoiding driving for fear of hitting pedestrians, driving very slowly	Driving near playgrounds, hospitals and care centers, mildly swerving car while driving near crosswalks, driving near shopping areas while playing loud music, no compulsive checking of the mirrors or road, driving at normal speed while saying feared phrases

Coordinating with other professionals who feel compelled to focus on risk

Sometimes you will need to coordinate care with other professionals who either fail to understand the implications of the OCD diagnosis or who believe it to be irresponsible to conduct ERP for harming OCD. As mentioned earlier, they may fail to understand that the diagnosis of harming OCD obviates the need for scrutiny of potential for harm. They might also be constrained by an interpretation of their professional responsibility that prioritizes risk management above clinical care, even when the risk is negligible. This can have iatrogenic effects on the patient and parents or even interfere with your treatment. I have several suggestions for managing this challenge.

First, be willing to go out of your way to communicate in person with those who fear for the safety of the patient or others. In-person communication gives you the opportunity to determine what the fear is that prevents the other from endorsing the diagnosis and treatment. You have a better opportunity to educate and hopefully allay their worries this way, as opposed to sending emails, texts or progress reports. Focus on identifying the specific worries and address those worries instead of assuming that misinformation about OCD is the problem. The strategy you might use for a nervous headmistress is different from what you might do when confronted with school policy. Be willing to state your case clearly, without hesitancy. For example, be willing to say, "There is no reason to fear that someone with harming OCD will hurt others or themselves. They will just be chronically anxious, miserable and at high risk for depression, under performance and a disabled life if they are not properly treated." Do not say, "Well, I can never promise anything for certain. Most people with harming OCD are harmless even though I have never heard of an exception." If an anxious administrator or healthcare professional is worried about care, then they need reassurance. You will only increase their uncertainty, and hence their anxiety, if you use vague phrases or hedging sentences.

If the issue is school policy, then be willing to assume the risk and find a way to help them meet their need for decreasing misperceived legal or other liability. I have been asked to write letters so patients can return to campus or be allowed to participate in various activities and I have been the one who says they no longer need continued risk assessment or referral to the Emergency Department. In this case, I write a letter or report clearly stating the problem is OCD and that in the future school staff or other professionals should follow my suggestions for implementing ERP and desist from risk assessment and referral to the Emergency Department. I make sure I inform others how to respond in an appropriate way, so they feel prepared with a suitable response. Here is a sample of this type of letter:

To whom it may concern,

I am writing on behalf of Abeba Smith, who was referred for evaluation of repeated suicidal ideation and possible suicidal behaviors. My assessment reveals that Abeba meets criteria for obsessive compulsive disorder (OCD) DSM 5, harming subtype, severe. Abeba gets unwanted intrusive thoughts about killing herself. She recognizes that these thoughts do not reflect her true intent and fears their presence means she might accidentally kill herself. She has been suffering from these intrusive thoughts for the past year. She has extensive avoidance in which she tries to avoid any situation in which she might be reminded of suicide or death and this interferes with listening to conversations, media, social media and classwork. She compulsively avoids anything she thinks she might use to harm herself and sleeps with her siblings in the hope they will prevent her from killing herself should she do that in her sleep. She has even slept with mittens on with taped wrists to keep herself from harming herself in her sleep.

Recently, after hearing about a suicide in a nearby school district, her fear increased, and she began touching a knife to her wrist to see if she would follow through with the impulse to kill herself or have no response. She was attempting to get rid of the uncertainty her intrusive thoughts provoked of "How do I know whether I will kill myself, even if I don't want to?" Each time she tried this experiment, her obsessions then played on her doubt and uncertainty by saying, "Since I didn't draw blood, how can I really know for sure I won't kill myself?" She ended up pressing the knife hard enough that it drew blood several times, until the point other girls in her physical education class noticed and informed your staff. At no time did she feel interested in self-harm or suicide. She was desperately attempting to alleviate anxiety caused by her intrusive thoughts.

Thus, it would best help her overcome her OCD if she is not again referred to the Emergency Department or suspended from school for an additional mental health evaluation should anyone notice evidence of compulsive behavior or thoughts of suicide. She does not meet criteria for any other diagnoses and has no history that places her at risk for suicide. Staff should refer any questions or concerns back to me at… Should staff notice or hear her talking about concerns about suicidal ideation or behaviors or see signs of potential self-harm, they should be instructed to say the following: "It looks as if your OCD is bothering you. What would your therapist tell you to do right now to help push back your OCD?" Showing a calm demeanor helps to reinforce the message her problem is overcoming OCD and not potential self-harm.

Your sincerely

If other professionals reject your diagnosis and treatment approach, then you need to be prepared to speak to the patient and family to make sure they understand and endorse your method of treatment. It is difficult for the patient to move forward when they are confused about what to believe and what to do. I explain the risk of giving in to the OCD by getting unnecessary reassurance in the form of professional evaluations, Emergency Department visits or crisis intervention. I have the patient and parents look at the effect doing this in the past has had on the OCD compared with not doing this by asking the following questions:

1. How much did you feel afraid of your thoughts before you... compared with after you...?

2. Did you feel stronger or weaker at ignoring your OCD after you...?

3. When you saw how worried everyone was and heard the kind of questions they asked, did it make you worry more about being dangerous or less?

4. Does ERP get easier or harder after you do...?

5. How much did you trust your opinion against OCD before... compared with after...?

These questions help to confirm the effect negative reinforcement and seeing the anxious way others react to intrusive thoughts has on worsening OCD. Most patients and parents will be able to recognize this pattern once you point it out and therefore better trust the process of ERP. It also helps to explain that school policy, liability issues or fear of lawsuits may be controlling how other professionals intervene to help the patient and parents, as they encourage a fear-driven risk-management approach to harming OCD.

Many teens and emerging adults can get stuck in the ritual of contacting crisis lines and school counselors or nurses to get a professional reaction to their intrusive thoughts. This necessitates response prevention practice in the form of a ban on Emergency Department visits, crisis calls and ad hoc visits to the school counselor or school. I set this up as part of the ERP plan and, whenever possible, make sure the others involved know how to respond by saying, "It looks as if your OCD is making you miserable. Talking to me is just going to make things worse. What exposure practice can you do right now to help get through this?" The patient earns rewards for avoiding talking to others about their intrusive thoughts and avoiding getting professional evaluation. Their goal is to learn to ignore the threatening content of the OCD and to carry on with their life.

Learning to ignore harming thoughts

Some patients need help to ignore their intrusive thoughts because even though they learn to do exposure and response prevention, they continue to fear that their thoughts indicate they have potential for danger. ERP, taking surveys to see how others think, and verification of the problem as being OCD do not seem to be enough to help these patients learn to look away when their intrusive thoughts occur. Training patients how to ignore their intrusive thoughts, as explained in Chapter 7, can be helpful. Some patients always get stuck when they try to analyze their intrusive thoughts. In this case, it is better to also use practice learning to redirect attention away from the OCD content while assuming it is just OCD. In my country, we have skunks that always spray a noxious odor which lasts for weeks when threatened. I liken attention redirection to learning to avoid kicking the skunk of OCD. If you kick a skunk, you will always get sprayed.

Now that you have covered ways to understand, evaluate and address difficult-to-treat subtypes of OCD, I will consider the very real problem of how to avoid burnout when working with these challenging cases.

If you would like to view a demonstration of how to implement some of the strategies mentioned in this chapter, please go to https://library.jkp.com/redeem using the code ZVEAZDD.

CHAPTER 10

Avoiding Therapist Fatigue when Working with Difficult Cases

The subtypes chosen for this book were selected because they are the ones that most vex mental health professionals and parents. If I am honest, the times when I am most likely to feel unsuccessful or frustrated by my lack of skill is when I encounter these OCD subtypes. If I think of the comments of my colleagues who are world class experts in OCD, these subtypes offer the same frustration for them as for everyone else. Unfortunately, the plain truth is that these subtypes are indeed likely to require more intervention of a more lengthy and complicated nature than easier-to-treat subtypes, such as contamination OCD. They require more nuance, persistence and patience. Although I have tried to be direct and simplify the concepts and treatment, I want to make clear that you are likely to spend many more sessions and more time in sessions with these patients as you help them. As I look back on my personal growth as a therapist and my years of supervising and training other mental health professionals, I see several common pitfalls in working with this population. I would like to mention these to help you avoid unnecessary fatigue, burnout or self-criticism and so you can find joy while working with these types of patients.

The pitfall of expecting too much

Many who work with OCD find it thrilling to see rapid progress in easier-to-treat OCD subtypes. They embrace ERP and OCD because progress can occur rapidly within a session and over a matter of a few weeks to months, unlike working with many other disorders. They accidentally develop the expectation based on experience that all cases of OCD will proceed similarly. Unfortunately, this is too often not the case with difficult-to-treat subtypes. It helps when working with the subtypes described in this book to assume a longer and more complicated course of treatment, regardless of your level of skill. It helps to reset your goals for smaller changes over a more gradual time, recognizing the limitations of intervention for this population. Many of the concepts necessary to succeed in treatment are complex, nuanced and difficult to understand for adults, let alone youth who are still developing moral reasoning, self-compassion and intellect. Treatment may entail teaching these skills simultaneously to teaching ERP skills. Thus, it helps to remind yourself that you are not alone in your struggle to help your patients and you are not failing because progress is slower or more erratic. You are paving the way for a better life for your patient and each small step forward is a big victory. You are the fortunate one who gets to set the stage for a better future.

The pitfall of doing too much by yourself

Patients with difficult-to-treat subtypes can be exhausting. Relentless reassurance seeking, compulsive analysis of past triggering experiences, and compulsive intolerance of uncertainty that makes the patient freeze and startle when you accidentally say something their OCD finds triggering can take its toll on every therapist. It is the reason I sometimes hear colleagues say, "How can you stand working with these patients?" If you are not careful, you can quickly become fatigued and overwhelmed by having to constantly be careful in your wording and how you respond so you avoid giving inappropriate reassurance or provoking so much anxiety that the patient gets stuck on a poorly worded explanation. One way I prevent professional fatigue is by working as part of an exposure team when doing intensive sessions at the start of treatment, holding sessions more than twice a week that last more than an hour. I am fortunate to have a team of staff who are all equally trained to work with OCD so we can each take one or two sessions a week while others fill in for the remainder of sessions. When I have been short of available staff, I have done the same with nearby colleagues in other practices who are trained in OCD treatment. This allows for more peer support, and commiseration when necessary, and enhances creativity when sharing ideas for advancing care. Commiserating with a colleague who has first-hand experience with the patient offers better support than explaining the situation to peers who are either unfamiliar with the patient or the experience of working with these subtypes of OCD. It's like being a combat veteran trying to explain to a civilian what being under fire is like. My suggestion is to avoid the temptation to do it all alone just because you are the resident OCD specialist at your clinic or the only one willing to take on the case. Feeling fresh and enthusiastic goes a long way toward improving your ability to stay calm, focused and creative.

The pitfall of trying to do treatment as usual

As mentioned in Chapter 1, weekly 45-minute sessions are often inadequate when working with difficult-to-treat subtypes of OCD. Frequently, the patient will be better served by an initial course of intensive treatment, which might not fit into your availability, your clinic's policy or the treatment allowed by the National Health Service, the family's finances, the patient's geographic location, or third-party payors. Many clinicians get stuck because they either assume they cannot be helpful due to these constraints, or they feel ineffective because they cannot offer the ideal treatment. My solution to this problem is to do two things: get creative and resourceful and remind myself that some treatment is better than no treatment. Being creative and resourceful means finding all possible other avenues where the patient and their family might access help, including live and online support groups, self-help media, youth camps sponsored by the International OCD Foundation and similar organizations, OCD conferences, parent support groups, low-cost telehealth, joining the International OCD Foundation, and getting your patient into residential, inpatient or intensive programs at other locations. You can increase accountability by having the patient text, email or call you with their daily ERP report on what happened during home practice. You could ask previously successful patients if they want to help as an exposure practice buddy for newer patients who share similar concerns. You can also train colleagues to help you when you are the sole therapist with OCD expertise. As previously mentioned, including the parents and significant others in treatment also improves the likelihood of follow through.

The general idea is to assume you are not alone and to locate the other resources that promote the perspective taking and ERP you are teaching the patient, so they have practice opportunities outside the time spent with you. Finally, you need to remind yourself that some skilful, accurate therapy that hits the target is much better than ineffective therapy offered in a large quantity. Although research shows the ideal treatment for OCD is to have a dose that matches severity, such as providing intensive ERP treatment, the slow route of less frequent but effective treatment can help the patient make forward steps. Like all other people who serve others, you must do the best you can with what you have while letting go of the disappointment you cannot offer more than you must give. This is still a gift to a patient and family who have failed at other treatment attempts or who have nowhere else to go. You really are good enough when armed with the knowledge from this book.

The pitfall of questioning the patient's or parent's motivation

Attribution bias states that we tend to attribute our own failings to the circumstances, and the failings of others to their poor character. We all fall victim to attribution bias unless we take care to train ourselves to view all human failings as the product of circumstance. The most common way I see therapists fall prey to attribution bias is to blame the parents. If the patient is a teen or emerging adult, then therapists are more likely to blame the patient. Be honest. How often have you thought or said, "Their mum is so difficult! No wonder my patient is so anxious," or, "They're so unmotivated. They never do their home practice," or, "They would do so much better if only their parents would make them do their home practice." Even if these statements might be factually true, they are corrosive to your professional joy. They suggest that you, the patient and the parents are powerless to overcome treatment-interfering behaviors. This will dampen your mood and creativity, misdirecting you away from viewing these issues as solvable problems. One of the things that makes working with young people so interesting, unlike adults who are more capable and likely self-referred, is the challenge of improving the community that surrounds the youth. When I run into cantankerous parents and patients, I remind myself to reframe their behavior as a product of their circumstances. Here are some helpful reframes that might also help you:

1. They cannot help themselves because their anxiety is overriding their ability to be polite and pleasant.

2. Their OCD is so overwhelming they are unable to listen well or grasp what I am saying.

3. Their child's OCD is overwhelming them and making them feel in crisis. No wonder they are so angry and demanding.

4. They are doing the best they can with what they have.

5. No one wants to live like this. They are just terrified of making things worse and that's why they cannot cooperate.

6. They are stuck in their fight, flight or freeze response and do not yet know it will always subside. That will just take practice.

7. Working with a mental health population always means that you are likely to encounter people with rough spots. It's just a normal day's work and not an insult or a crisis.

8. If this child were an animal, they would be biting me instead of saying ugly things. Thank goodness they are only a scared human!

The pitfall of failing to pivot and be flexible when the patient refuses

When doing behavioral interventions, we are often taught to stick to the plan and work through each step before heading to the next. For example, you explain the disorder, set up a range of exposure tasks and response prevention tasks, start with easier things to build confidence when possible or with imaginal exposure and then do in vivo exposure. What do you do, however, when the patient is unable to do particular exposure practices, or always gives in with compulsions? I have offered various strategies throughout this book to address this problem. Unfortunately, even your best efforts might result in outright refusal or constant undoing of the exposure task by mental rituals or rituals done after the session. Many therapists get stuck, believing either they cannot proceed in treatment, or they have difficulty coming up with alternative ways to accomplish the task. Sometimes the way to manage this situation is by asking the patient, "What would make it a half step or tiny bit easier to do the exposure?" It might mean delaying the compulsive response in tiny increments, such as seconds. In other instances, it might mean you have gone as far as possible with your treatment and need to find other ways to augment treatment with medication, transcranial magnetic stimulation, supplements or facilities that can do more intensive treatment or other alternative treatments. My advice is to go to the website of the International OCD Foundation listed in the Resources section to find the latest information on new trends in alternative treatments. When the best-proven treatments have been unsuccessful, it makes sense to try any reasonable option that is likely to work. Getting stuck in a particular theoretical zone or the theory in which you were trained will dampen your ability to be resourceful. OCD can be a horrible disorder that ruins lives. Our patients deserve our intellectual honesty and willingness to seek out new options we may not feel well versed in or even understand. I have had patients find additional relief with neurosurgery, novel medications, transcranial magnetic stimulation, supplements, CBD oil (cannabidiol oil with the THC component removed), acupuncture, vagal nerve stimulation and more. Be willing to assume there is much more to be learned about OCD by keeping abreast of new developments. New developments are often the very thing that can give difficult-to-treat patients the extra advantage.

In summary, I am grateful for your willingness to satisfy your curiosity by reading this book. Your commitment to alleviate the suffering of your patients who suffer from OCD blesses those you serve. I hope I have inspired you to refine your skills, so you feel more confident when faced with challenging cases of OCD. Your willingness to be persistent, creative and patient will give your patients greater opportunity to live free from the shackles of mistaken self-doubt, intolerance of uncertainty and pointless compulsions. May you be blessed on your journey as a healer of OCD.

Resources

General

Brown, T. & Barlow, D. (1994) Anxiety and Related Disorders Interview Schedule for DSM-5 (ADIS-5)® Child Version and Parent Version. Oxford University Press. The ADIS-5 is an easy-to-use structured clinical interview you can order online.

International OCD Foundation has information about OCD and PANS: https://iocdf.org/search/PANS

PANDAS Physicians Network provides up-to-date scientific information on the diagnosis and treatment of these disorders. It has a list of international providers who specialize in the treatment of PANS/PANDAS: www.pandasppn.org

The Gottman Foundation has easy-to-read articles for patients and professionals. It explains the science behind healthy and rewarding couples relationships: www.gottman.com

Scrupulous Anonymous is particularly useful for Catholic, Anglican and Lutheran patients who suffer from scrupulosity. I recommend looking up the Scrupulous Anonymous Five Simple Truths and the Ten Commandments for the Scrupulous: https://scrupulousanonymous.org

For Christians with scrupulosity

Santa, T.M. (2007) *Understanding Scrupulosity: Questions, Helps & Encouragement*. Liguori, MO: Liguori Publications.

Van Ornum, W. (1997) *A Thousand Frightening Fantasies: Understanding and Healing Scrupulosity and Obsessive Compulsive Disorder*. Eurgene, OR: Wipft & Stock Publishers.

Ciarrocchi, J. (1995) *The Doubting Disease: Help for Scrupulosity and Religious Compulsions*. New York, NY: Integration Books.

For Jews with scrupulosity

Bonchek, A. (2009) *Religious Compulsions & Fears: A Guide to Treatment*. New York, NY: Philipp Feldheim.

Gard, R. (1962) *Judaism: The Unity of the Jewish Spirit throughout the Ages*. New York, NY: Braziller.

For Buddhists with scrupulosity

Gard, R. (1962) *Buddhism: The Way of Buddhism*. New York, NY: Braziller.

For Muslims with scrupulosity

Gard, R. (1962) *Islam: The Tradition and Contemporary Orientation of Islam*. New York, NY: Braziller.

Brief summary of basic faith concepts

Christianity

Any child or adult who acknowledges that Jesus Christ is God (the proof being his resurrection after being crucified by the Romans) and who understands they are imperfect and always at risk to do things that lead to human suffering (called Original Sin) is a Christian in God's good grace. Those who accept the concept that Christ was the permanent sacrifice that bridges the gap between human innate sinfulness and God's perfect love are forgiven without any requirement other than they become baptized. God is understood to be constantly forgiving of anyone who acknowledges their inability to be perfectly good. God also regards all people, whether Christian or not, with love, whether or not they acknowledge God. Those who love God are promised an afterlife of living in the presence of a perfectly loving God and all others who similarly believe in Jesus' divinity. Those who fail to seek God or who deny the presence of God will suffer an afterlife of permanent absence from God's loving presence. Thus, anyone who is a Christian accepts they can never do anything perfectly and is absolved of the need to attain perfection of faith or good behaviors. Good works are understood to be an expression of gratitude for God's love and an extension of God's love through Christians in the world. Good intentions and good behavior are never a means to gain God's favor or an afterlife with God. Here are relevant holy scriptures that express these concepts:

> "Teacher, which is the greatest commandment in the Law?" Jesus replied: "Love the Lord your God with all your heart and with all your soul and with all your mind." This is the first and greatest commandment. And the second is like it: "Love your neighbor as yourself." All the Law and the Prophets hang on these two commandments. (Matthew 22:36–40, NIV)

> For it is by grace you have been saved, through faith—and this is not from yourselves, it is the gift of God not by works, so that no one can boast. (Ephesians 2:8–9, NIV)

Judaism

Jews view sin as an expression of the yetzer hara, which "is a debasement of man's proper nature. Punishment is therefore not primarily retribution: it is chastisement, as a father chastises his children, to remind them of their proper dignity and character. Repentance is therefore in Hebrew, Teshuva, returning, man's turning back to his truest nature" (Gard, 1962, p.195). Mitzvahs are the acts of goodness that draw people closer to God and each other. God forgives those who seek to be close to God, and to acknowledge the effects of their yetzer hara all Jews are expected to seek atonement by fasting and praying during Yom Kippur (Reconstructing Judaism, April 8, 2016). There-fore, repentance simply means returning to following the rules of the Torah according to one's congregation. Mitsvahs do not control God's response to people but instead reflect the true nature of mankind.

Rabbis, Jewish clergy, have authority to issue dispensations to relax rules of observance to accommodate circumstance, such as illness, age or mental illness. The only rules that may not be relaxed are the requirement to fast for a full day on Yom Kippur and Rosh Hashanah. More conservative congregations may also require fasting on other holidays. Scrupulosity OCD is therefore understood to be a mental illness and rabbis routinely endorse treatment, including exposure with response prevention.

Islam

Followers of Islam are instructed to assume that God is merciful and will always forgive anyone who requests forgiveness. Followers are also instructed to live a good life, just as Jews and Christians are. Good works do not improve God's disposition toward the follower. Feeling hopeless of God's mercy is prohibited. Scrupulosity OCD symptoms, therefore, are viewed as a problem of mental health rather than an expression of religious observance. The following are relevant holy writings to assist you in treatment:

> O son of Adam, so long as you call on Me, and ask of Me, I shall forgive you for what you have done, and I shall not mind. (*Hadith Qudse*)

> O my Servants who have transgressed against their souls! Despair not of the Mercy of Allah: for Allah forgives all sins: for He is Oft-Forgiv-ing, Most Merciful. (*Quran, Sura 39 (Az-Zumar), ayah 53*)

> O son of Adam, so long as you call on Me, and ask of Me, I shall forgive you for what you have done, and I shall not mind. O son of Adam, were your sins to reach the clouds of the sky and were you then to ask forgiveness of Me, I would forgive you. O son of Adam, were you to come to Me with sins nearly as great as the earth, and were you then to face Me, ascribing no partner to Me, I would bring you forgiveness nearly as great as it. (*Hadith Qudse*)

Buddhism

All beings are understood to be in a constant cycle of learning through life experience on a state of continual reincarnation into higher or lower life forms that depends on their willingness to learn the lessons of good morality in their current life. As beings ascend into higher life forms, they bear greater moral responsibility for their intentions and behavior. Current suffering is understood to be the product of wrong expectation, past misdeeds and failure to cultivate virtue in the current life. Act of goodness and living a life that "abstain(s) from killing living beings, stealing, sexual misconduct, lying and intoxication" is the goal for humans in their current life (Salim, 2020). Being compassionate, engaging in acts of kindness, avoiding use of alcohol or recreational drugs, being of service to all beings and letting go of expectation and materialism are virtues that lead to reincarnation as a higher life form. If one successfully evolves repeatedly through the higher life forms, then one can attain Nirvana, a state of perfect knowledge, compassion and bliss. Thus, the individual bears the burden of their bad behavior and lack of virtue in both the current and future life (Gard, 1962). There is no permanent last chance that dooms someone because of misdeeds, only the present and future opportunity to learn and grow into a more highly evolved being. Thus, all beings have an infinite number of "do overs." There are also many ways to counter the effects of bad behavior and evil intention through prayer, acts of devotion and service. You can compensate for misdeeds. Compassion, humility and lack of anger are heavily emphasized as virtues to cultivate. It would be incorrect to do harmful things to oneself or others or to engage in behaviors that make it impossible to live a life of compassion and service. Therefore, scrupulous thought and behavior would be understood to be a meaningless waste of time that could be otherwise spent in virtuous behavior (Gard, 1962).

The Buddha is understood to be completely evolved into a state of Nirvana and is a divine being who regards all with perfect compassion, good humor and understanding. Those who are religious leaders or lamas are understood to be reincarnations of Buddha or other fully evolved beings. Lamas, therefore, are exemplars of great wisdom, compassion and knowledge and often possess miraculous skills, such as the Buddha demonstrated. Their writings often have great psychological insights relating to compassion, forgiveness and humility and can be useful when a patient's compulsions prevent the patient from living a well life.

> Love and compassion are necessities, not luxuries. Without them, humanity cannot survive... Our prime purpose in this life is to help others. And if you can't help them, at least don't hurt them. (Dalai Lama, February 12, 2019)

As you can see from a brief summary of four major world religions, no matter what scrupulosity may impose, it is incorrect for any patient to believe they have made a fatal and unforgivable mistake that dooms them for all eternity. Each religion heavily emphasizes becoming a person who is capable of great compassion. Each religion has ways to manage and overcome failures in character that are attainable while allowing for human imperfection. None of these religions advocates self-harm in the manner of penance, separation from God due to unworthiness once you are a member of the community or the idea that a member of the community could invoke eternal permanent harm through their misdeeds. This is important to know because most patients with scrupulosity have obsessions that relate to the worst-case scenario of being unable to attain God's favor or of shaming themselves through their inability to attain perfection in thought, intention or deed.

References

American Psychiatric Association (2022) *Diagnostic and Statistical Manual of Mental Disorders, Fifth Edition* (DSM-V). Washington, DC: American Psychiatric Association.

Baillie, A.J. & Rapee, R.A. (2005) Panic attacks as risk markers for mental disorders. *Social Psychiatry and Psychiatric Epidemiology*, 40: 240–244. PMID: 15742230; PMCID: PMC6300830.

Barlow, D.H., Farchione, T.J., Bullis, J.R., Gallagher, M.W. *et al.* (2017) The unified protocol for transdiagnostic treatment of emotional disorders compared with diagnosis-specific protocols for anxiety disorders: A randomized clinical trial. *JAMA Psychiatry*, 74(9): 875–884. doi: 10.1001/jamapsychiatry.2017.2164. PMID: 28768327; PMCID: PMC5710228.

Barrera, T.L. & Norton, P.J. (2011) The appraisal of intrusive thoughts in relation to obsessional-compulsive symptoms. *Cognitive Behavior Therapy*, 40(2): 98–110. doi: 10.1080/16506073.2010.545072. PMID: 21491252.

Brakoulias, V., Starcevic, V., Berle, D., Milicevic, D. *et al.* (2013) The characteristics of unacceptable/taboo thoughts in obsessive-compulsive disorder. *Comprehensive Psychiatry*, 54(7): 750–757. doi: 10.1016/j.comppsych.2013.02.005. PMID: 23587527.

Brand, S. & Kirov, R. (2011) Sleep and its importance in adolescence and in common adolescent somatic and psychiatric conditions. *International Journal of General Medicine*, 4: 425–442. doi: 10.2147/IJGM.S11557. PMID: 21731894; PMCID: PMC3119585.

Brown, K., Farmer, C., Farhadian, B., Hernandez, J., Thienemann, M. & Frankovich, J. (2017) Pediatric acute-onset neuropsychiatric syndrome response to oral corticosteroid bursts: An observational study of patients in an academic community-based PANS clinic. *Journal of Child and Adolescent Psychopharmacology*, 27(7): 629–639. doi: 10.1089/cap.2016.0139. PMID: 28714753; PMCID: PMC5749576.

Cabrera, J.F. & Kwon, R. (2018) Income inequality, household income, and mass shooting in the United States. *Frontiers in Public Health*, 17(6): 294. doi: 10.3389/fpubh.2018.00294. PMID: 30386762; PMCID: PMC6199901.

Camilleri, C., Perry, J.T. & Sammut, S. (2020) Compulsive internet pornography use and mental health: A cross-sectional study in a sample of university students in the United States. *Frontiers in Psychology*, 12(11): 613244. doi: 10.3389/fpsyg.2020.613244. PMID: 33510691; PMCID: PMC7835260.

Cassiday, K.L (2022) *The No Worries Guide to Helping Your Anxious Child: A Handbook to Help You and Your Anxious Child Thrive*. London: Jessica Kingsley Publishers.

Ciarrocchi, J. (1995) *The Doubting Disease: Help for Scrupulosity and Religious Compulsions*. New York, NY: Integration Books.

Cornell, D., Guerra, N., Kincherff, R., Williamson, M.A. *et al.* (2022) Gun Violence: Prediction, Prevention, and Policy. American Psychological Association. www.apa.org/pubs/reports/gun-violence-prevention.

Duckworth, A.L., Kirby, T.A., Tsukayama, E., Berstein, H. & Ericsson, K.A. (2011) Deliberate practice spells success: Why grittier competitors triumph at the National Spelling Bee. *Social Psychological and Personality Science*, 2(2): 174–181. doi: 10.1177/1948550610385872.

Endres, D., Pollak, T.A., Bechter, K., Denzel, D. *et al.* (2022) Immunological causes of obsessive-compulsive disorder: Is it time for the concept of an "autoimmune OCD" subtype? *Translational Psychiatry*, 12(1): 5. doi: 10.1038/s41398-021-01700-4. PMID: 35013105; PMCID: PMC8744027.

Ericsson, K.A., Krampe, R.T. & Tesch-Römer, C. (1993) The role of deliberate practice in the acquisition of expert performance. *Psychological Review*, 100(3): 363–406. doi:10.1037/0033-295X.100.3.363.

Fineberg, N.A., Hollander, E., Pallanti, S., Walitza, S. *et al.* (2020) Clinical advances in obsessive-compulsive disorder: A position statement by the International College of Obsessive-Compulsive Spectrum Disorders. *International Clinical Psychopharmacology*, 35(4): 173–193. doi: 10.1097/YIC.0000000000000314. PMID: 32433254; PMCID: PMC7255490.

Frankovich, J. (2022) Post-infectious inflammatory brain disorders and PANS/PANDAS: A discussion with Jennifer Frankovich, MD, MS. www.pandasppn.org/frankovich-discussion.

Gard, R. (1962) *Judaism: The Unity of the Jewish Spirit throughout the Ages*. New York, NY: Braziller.

Gottman, J. & Silver, N. (2015) *The Seven Principles for Making Marriage Work: A Practical Guide from the Country's Foremost Expert*. New York, NY: Harmony Books.

Greenberg, D. & Huppert, J.D. (2010) Scrupulosity: A unique subtype of Obsessive-Compulsive Disorder. *Current Psychiatry Reports*, 12: 282–289. doi:10.1007/s11920-010-0127-5.

Grisham, J.R., Fullana, M.A., Mataix-Cols, D., Moffitt, T.E., Caspi, A. & Poulton, R. (2011) Risk factors prospectively associated with adult obsessive-compulsive symptom dimensions and obsessive-compulsive disorder. *Psychological Medicine*, 41(12): 2495–2506. doi: 10.1017/ S0033291711000894. PMID: 21672296.

Harrington, M.O., Ashton, J.E., Sankarasubramanian, S., Anderson, M.C. & Cairney, S.A. (2021) Losing control: Sleep deprivation impairs the suppression of unwanted thoughts. *Clinical Psychological Science*, 9(1): 97–113. doi: 10.1177/2167702620951511. PMID: 33552705; PMCID: PMC7820573.

James, S.C., Farrell, L.J. & Zimmer-Gembeck, M. (2017) Description and Prevalence of OCD in Children and Adolescents. In J.A. Abramowitz, D. McKay & E. Storch (eds), *The Wiley Handbook of Obsessive Compulsive Disorders* (pp.5–23). New York, NY: Wiley Blackwell. https://doi. org/10.1002/9781118890233.

Jones, J. (2022) Belief in God in US Dips to 81%, a New Low. Gallup: Politics, June. https://news.gallup.com/poll/393737/belief-god-dips-new-low. aspx.

Lebois, L.A.M., Seligowski, A.V., Wolff, J.D., Hill, S.B. & Ressler, K.J. (2019) Augmentation of extinction and inhibitory learning in anxiety and trauma-related disorders. *Annual Review of Clinical Psychology*, 7(15): 257–284. doi: 10.1146/annurev-clinpsy-050718-095634. PMID: 30698994; PMCID: PMC6547363.

Lebowitz, E.R., Marin, C., Martino, A., Shimshoni, Y. & Silverman, W.K. (2020) Parent-based treatment as efficacious as cognitive-behavioral therapy for childhood anxiety: A randomized noninferiority study of supportive parenting for anxious childhood emotions. *Journal of the American Academy of Child and Adolescent Psychiatry*, 59(3): 362–372. doi: 10.1016/j.jaac.2019.02.014. PMID: 30851397; PMCID: PMC6732048.

Loftus, E.F. (1996) Memory distortion and false memory creation. *Bulletin of the American Academy of Psychiatry and Law*, 24(3): 281–295. PMID: 8889130.

Lowe, S.R. & Galea, S. (2017) The mental health consequences of mass shootings. *Trauma, Violence, & Abuse*, 18(1): 62–82. doi: 10.1177/1524838015591572. PMID: 26084284.

Lundström, S., Forsman, M., Larsson, H., Kerekes, N. *et al.* (2014) Childhood neurodevelopmental disorders and violent criminality: A sibling control study. *Journal of Autism Development Disorders*, 44(11): 2707–2716. doi: 10.1007/s10803-013-1873-0. PMID: 23807203.

Mattebo, M., Tydén, T., Häggström-Nordin, E., Nilsson, K.W. & Larsson, M. (2018) Pornography consumption and psychosomatic and depressive symptoms among Swedish adolescents: A longitudinal study. *Upsala Journal of Medical Sciences*, 123(4): 237–246. doi: 10.1080/03009734.2018.1534907. PMID: 30411651; PMCID: PMC6327603.

McClellan, J. (2018) Psychosis in children and adolescents. *Journal of the American Academy of Child and Adolescent Psychiatry*, 57(5): 308–312. doi: 10.1016/j.jaac.2018.01.021. PMID: 29706159.

McCoy, K. (2022) Intersectionality in pandemic youth suicide attempt trends. *Suicide and Life-Threatening Behavior*, 52(5): 983–993. doi: 10.1111/sltb.12895. PMID: 35735265.

Morgenroth, T., Ryan, M.K. & Peters, K. (2015) The motivational theory of role modeling: How role models influence role aspirants' goals. *Review of General Psychology*, 19(4): 465–483. doi: 10.1037/gpr0000059.

Monzani, B., Vidal-Ribas, P., Turner, C., Krebs, G. *et al.* (2020) The role of paternal accommodation of paediatric OCD symptoms: Patterns and implications for treatment outcomes. *Journal of Abnormal Child Psychology*, 48(10): 1313–1323. doi: 10.1007/s10802-020-00678-9. PMID: 32683586; PMCID: PMC7445192.

O'Connor, E.E., Holly, L.E., Chevalier, L.L., Pincus, D.B. & Langer, D.A. (2020) Parent and child emotion and distress responses associated with parental accommodation of child anxiety symptoms. *Journal of Clinical Psychology*, 76(7): 1390–1407. doi: 10.1002/jclp.22941. PMID: 32060945; PMCID: PMC7282941.

O'Dor, S.L., Zagaroli, J.S., Belisle, R.M., Hamel, M.A. *et al.* (2022) The COVID-19 pandemic and children with PANS/PANDAS: An evaluation of symptom severity, telehealth, and vaccination hesitancy. *Child Psychiatry & Human Development*, 5: 1–9. doi: 10.1007/s10578-022-01401-z. Epub ahead of print. PMID: 35930178; PMCID: PMC9361990.

O'Kearney, R.T., Anstey, K.J. & von Sanden, C. (2006) Behavioural and cognitive behavioural therapy for obsessive compulsive disorder in children and adolescents. *Cochrane Database Systems Review*, 18; 2006(4): CD004856. doi: 10.1002/14651858.CD004856.pub2. PMID: 17054218; PMCID: PMC8855344.

Pittenger, C., Kelmendi, B., Bloch, M., Krystal, J.H. & Coric, V. (2005) Clinical treatment of obsessive-compulsive disorder. *Psychiatry (Edgmont)*, 2(11): 34–43. PMID: 21120095; PMCID: PMC2993523.

Rahman, F., Webb, R.T. & Wittkowski, A. (2021) Risk factors for self-harm repetition in adolescents: A systematic review. *Clinical Psychology Review*, 88: 102048. doi: 10.1016/j.cpr.2021.102048. PMID: 34119893.

Ramirez Basco, M., Bostic, J., Davies, D., Rush, A.J., Witte, B., Hendrickse, W. & Barnett, V. (2000) Methods to improve diagnostic accuracy in a community mental health setting. *American Journal of Psychiatry*, 157(10), 1599–1605. doi: 10.1176/appi.ajp.157.10.1599. PMID: 11007713.

Reconstructing Judaism (2016, April 8). www.reconstructingjudaism.org.

Ruch, D.A., Sheftall, A.H., Schlagbaum, P., Rausch, J., Campo, J.V. & Bridge, J.A. (2019) Trends in suicide among youth aged 10 to 19 years in the United States, 1975 to 2016. *JAMA Network Open*, 2(5): e193886. doi:

10.1001/jamanetworkopen.2019.3886. Erratum in: *JAMA Network Open,* 2(6): e197687. PMID: 31099867; PMCID: PMC6537827.

Salim, A.R. (2020) *Islam Explained: A Short Introduction to History, Teachings, and Culture.* Emeryville, CA: Rockridge Press.

Shafran, R. & Rachman, S. (2004) Thought-action fusion: A review. *Journal of Behavior Therapy and Experimental Psychiatry,* 35(2): 87 107.

Sharma, E., Sharma, L.P., Balachander, S., Lin, B. *et al.* (2021) Comorbidities in Obsessive-Compulsive Disorder across the lifespan: A systematic review and meta-analysis. *Frontiers in Psychiatry,* 11(12): 703701. doi: 10.3389/fpsyt.2021.703701. PMID: 34858219; PMCID: PMC8631971.

Shobhana, S.S. & Raviraj, K.G. (2022) Global trends of suicidal thought, suicidal ideation, and self-harm during COVID-19 pandemic: A systematic review. *Egyptian Journal of Forensic Sciences,* 12, 28. doi:10.1186/s41935-022-00286-2.

Strawn, J.R., Lu, L., Peris, T.S., Levine, A. & Walkup, J.T. (2021) Research Review: Pediatric anxiety disorders—what have we learnt in the last 10 years? *Journal of Child Psychology and Psychiatry,* 62(2): 114–139. doi: 10.1111/jcpp.13262. PMID: 32500537; PMCID: PMC7718323.

Tamir, C., Connaughton, A. & Salazar, A.M. (2020) *The Global God Divide.* Report. Pew Research Center. www.pewresearch.org/global/2020/07/20/the-global-god-divide.

Tümkaya, S., Karadağ, F., Yenigün, E.H., Özdel, O. & Kashyap, H. (2018) Metacognitive beliefs and their relation with symptoms in obsessive-compulsive disorder. *Noro Psikiyatr Ars,* 55(4): 358–363. doi: 10.29399/npa.22655.

Walter, H.J., Bukstein, O.G., Abright, A.R., Keable, H. *et al.* (2020) Clinical practice guideline for the assessment and treatment of children and adolescents with anxiety disorders. *Journal of the American Academy of Child and Adolescent Psychiatry,* 59(10): 1107–1124. doi: 10.1016/j.jaac.2020.05.005. PMID: 32439401.

Wehry, A.M., Beesdo-Baum, K., Hennelly, M.M., Connolly, S.D. & Strawn, J.R. (2015) Assessment and treatment of anxiety disorders in children and adolescents. *Current Psychiatry Reports,* 17(7): 52. doi: 10.1007/s11920-015-0591-z. PMID: 25980507; PMCID: PMC4480225.

Williams, M.T., Farris, S.G., Turkheimer, E.N., Franklin, M.E. *et al.* (2014) The impact of symptom dimensions on outcome for exposure and ritual prevention therapy in obsessive-compulsive disorder. *Journal of Anxiety Disorders,* 28(6): 553–558. doi: 10.1016/j.janxdis.2014.06.001. PMID: 24983796; PMCID: PMC4151097.

Zimmer-Gembeck, M. & Helfand, M. (2008) Ten years of longitudinal research on U.S. adolescent sexual behavior: Developmental correlates of sexual intercourse, and the importance of age, gender and ethnic background. *Developmental Review,* 28(2): 153–224. doi: 10.1016/j.dr.2007.06.001.

Index